PREVENTING
POLARIZATION

50 **STRATEGIES** FOR TEACHING KIDS ABOUT EMPATHY, POLITICS, AND CIVIC RESPONSIBILITY

MICHELLE BLANCHET   BRIAN DETERS

Preventing Polarization
© 2023 by Times 10 Publications
Highland Heights, OH 44143 USA
Website: 10publications.com

All web links in this book are correct as of the publication date but may have become inactive or otherwise modified since that time.

Cover and Interior Design by Steven Plummer
Project Management by Jen Z. Marshall
Editing by Chris O'Byrne
Copyediting by Jennifer Jas
Paperback ISBN: 978-1-956512-27-4
eBook ISBN: 978-1-956512-28-1
Hardcover ISBN: 978-1-956512-29-8
Library of Congress Cataloging-in-Publication Data is available for this title.

For our children.

And to all the grown-ups out there working to ensure they leave our youth with the world a little better off than how they found it.

"It's easier to build strong children than to repair broken adults."

— FREDERICK DOUGLASS

TABLE OF CONTENTS

WHY WE NEED TO STOP AVOIDING CIVICS AND POLITICS

MAGINE IT'S THE holidays and your family has gathered in person for the first time in a year. Most conversations are going fine, but clear tension exists between your uncle and your cousin because of a fiery Facebook clash the two had last week over the latest political controversy. Inevitably, a few hours into the day, the argument explodes into a yelling match while Mom tries to distract them by passing the sweet potatoes around the table.

The rest of the family awkwardly reacts by either sitting silently or attempting to change the subject. Everyone eats their dessert in agitation, waiting for the next wave of arguments. And through all this tension and arguing, nothing productive comes out of it. The result of this holiday debacle is that the two "unfriend" each other on Facebook, and the rest of the family avoids having any controversial talks for fear of another family fallout.

Who can relate to this scenario?

It's fair to say that American culture discourages discussing religion or politics. We tend to avoid ideological conflicts, but ignoring them doesn't make them go away. The consequence is that we've now become a nation that can no longer discuss religion and politics civilly. We've become a divided nation, which no one wants, and the situation is counterproductive to meeting the needs of people.

The word "politics" has become tainted as a negative concept. Issues have become highly polarized, and we cannot move forward on even the most pressing topics. Compounding this division are the labels we put on people by their beliefs and our prejudices, making it nearly impossible to communicate effectively. The damage from this has caused such destruction that we can no longer entertain constructive discourses to find solutions to the problems we face.

However, we have more in common than we're led to believe. We have a world filled with smart, talented, and kind people who all have the same needs: love, health, acceptance, and belonging. Almost everyone wants the best for their families and communities, but the fact that we can't have a dialogue anymore, that we've cut communication, is causing us to become even more divided. It's debilitating for many, and the only way to heal is to open the lines of communication once more. We need to take back our ability to speak to one another with civility and to go beyond the same old rhetoric that follows each issue. We need to allow people to think critically about how we might address the multitude of problems that weigh our nation.

As teachers ourselves, we see education as the path forward. But we know that a one-off civics course will not be enough to get the job done. That's why we're calling on our colleagues, all the teachers out there of all grade levels and subject areas (and parents, too), to help encourage civic-mindedness. We all can contribute by helping our students develop the building blocks they need to be good and responsible citizens who can build a future in which they want to live.

This may sound big—unachievable, even—but when you think about it, isn't that the point of school? Aren't schools supposed to raise young people who turn into responsible adults who can make intelligent decisions about our world and communities? We all can do more to contribute to this cause, and it's not as hard as you might think.

From our experience teaching civics, we've been on a quest to figure out what's causing the communication breakdown we're seeing and what we could do in our civics courses to bring the conversation back to where it needs to be. As we've analyzed social media clashes; poorly conducted news debates; and the dialogues of friends, colleagues, and neighbors, we've discovered many reasons why communication is at an all-time low, and polarization is on the rise. But we've also uncovered many ways we might open the roadblocks hindering the dialogue we so desperately need so people might come together to find consensus.

To help our students understand the essence of civics, why it matters, and why their engagement is so critical to its success, we uncover the skills we need to nurture in our students to produce more engaged citizens. In the pages you're about to explore, you'll find strategies to help build these skills. We have ensured that these ideas are basic enough so any teacher can apply them to their content and practice.

Why any teacher? Can't just civics teachers do this? Isn't that their job?

Honestly, that's the problem. Most civics courses right now only teach the role of government and how it functions. Make your way into a typical civics or government classroom in "Anywhere, USA," and you are likely to find endless lessons on facts like the functions of the three branches, the constitutional qualifications of our government officials, and an examination of the structure of federalism, but you'll probably find very little on the politics that shape those frameworks.

To avoid confrontation, we avoid discussing what the government should do. The result is that students are not equipped to discuss tough issues. Living in a country where learning about civics seems positive but being political is negative, we've found ourselves in a dilemma. What's the point of learning about the rights and duties of citizenship, the definition of civics, when our culture frowns on being political and students turn into adults without the desire or skills to be productive political citizens in a democracy?

We need your help to change the rhetoric.

This book is not about civics, at least not directly. It is about taking simple steps so students are prepared to engage in civics and politics as young people and adults. It is about building consensus and learning effective ways to understand and communicate with one another. Through these steps, we firmly believe students will be on a path to have tough conversations (with people they may not even agree with), to get proactive on challenges, and to find constructive ways to be engaged and informed citizens who bring about needed commonality.

As you look through the chapters and skillbuilders in these pages, you'll notice that you can personalize and differentiate these actions based on your classroom content and the opportunities available to you. We've focused on the skills students need to be civically minded, and there's more than one path to get to the destination.

Thank you for taking this journey with us.

HOW TO USE THIS BOOK

If you're reading this book, you're probably well aware of the polarization that is happening in many countries. This book is not an analysis of those divisions. In *Preventing Polarization*, we've prioritized ten skills that any teacher (or parent) could employ in the classroom (or home) that promote constructive dialogues, civic-mindedness, and (hopefully) engaged adults who can work together and find consensus to solve the world's many challenges.

Each strategy operates as a standalone initiative. Work on one. Take a break and come back when you're ready to try out another. The material in this book is actionable, and you can apply it to teaching. It might also serve as a source of standalone activities you can do with students (or your children). As you read through each skill, here's the framework of what you'll uncover:

- **The Problem:** The introduction of each section discusses why we picked the selected skill. This is our "aha" moment as to how neglecting this skill might lead to polarization.

- **The Solution:** We make an argument for how nurturing this skill in our youth and in others will help alleviate the communication breakdown we're seeing.

- **Civics Connection:** This section is geared more directly to the civics classroom and describes how neglecting the skill impacts our students. As civics teachers, we see how the lack of certain skills prevents us from cultivating civic-mindedness and acts as a barrier to teaching the subject. We're the last line of defense for many students in our quest to develop civic-minded adults. At the moment, sadly but truthfully, we're collectively failing in this effort.

- **Make This Skill a Reality:** Here, you'll find an outline of what the strategy might look like in a classroom or home, how it benefits students, and the outcomes you might see. We offer conceptual information to help you nurture or build the specific skill for yourself or others.

- **Strategies You Can Implement Right Away:** This section includes five ideas, activities, and strategies you can act on immediately, for a total of fifty strategies in this book. Please use and share them.

As with all these skillbuilders, the first step toward developing them in our students is to make them a priority. Too often, our curriculum ignores how we might teach certain skills (especially those that enhance our emotional intelligence), so it's easier to put these off. Civic-mindedness is not just a life skill; it's a mindset that will shape our entire society.

Given its importance, everyone should be involved in this initiative. We have ample opportunities to develop these skills—in ourselves and in our students—through a wide range of outlets. It's in how we model our behavior, the pedagogy we employ, the types of assessments we demand, and the standards we set. We must hold ourselves accountable for ensuring that our youth understand what matters and that they have a responsibility to take care of our country and our future when the time comes.

While this book is full of ideas about how you might incorporate these skills, we understand they're not the final solution. We trust you, as teachers and parents, to figure out how to incorporate these ideas and skills in a way that works best for you. We welcome your ingenuity as we all work together on this important mission. In the Appendix, we've included a *"Design Your Own Activity"* template. It's a step-by-step guide to DIY your initiative to employ a strategy in your classroom. Use this as you brainstorm or just do your thing. All we ask is that you do something positive. Every action matters. Every step counts.

WHAT THIS BOOK IS NOT

Before we get into the detailed purposes of what this book is about, we also need to address even more what this book is *not* about.

In short, we are not writing this to explore and analyze *why* we have become polarized in so many pockets of the world. We are here to point out the obvious: *the milk has spilled*, and we need to clean it up. We might mention various polarizing ingredients in the upcoming pages, but it's not our intent to discuss why these have come about or to what degree; instead, we aim to share guidance on the strategies you can implement to assure the next generation doesn't fall into the same patterns.

Please do not assume the current polarization is because the skills we suggest were not being employed before. We have no way of knowing to what degree we have used or neglected these strategies in the past. Our experience leads us to believe they are worthwhile to try and might help get us back on the right track.

It is worthwhile to briefly mention a few key ingredients that make polarization such a difficult problem.

- *Misinformation.* For example, the evolutionary framework of our social media platforms produces a tremendous amount of misinformation. This misinformation is so saturating that it has led to many people not knowing what to believe. People magnify this post-truth reality when they drift into their tribal algorithmic patterns of information. The problem gets compounded when we stop trusting our institutions and those working for them.

- *Ego.* Studies like the Dunning-Kruger effect have explored and scientifically determined that people develop certainty in what they digest if they have less information on a subject than if they have more information. We are here to assure that misinformation doesn't have to detrimentally impact kids today—like it has many of their parents—if they are exposed to these skills.

- *Tribalism.* Identity politics and bumper sticker politics have played into the disconnect we all feel and experience. This book isn't about trying to sort out how we have become tribal; it's a book about trying to help end tribalism in the future.

- *VUCA.* VUCA stands for *volatility, uncertainty, complexity, and ambiguity* and is necessary to understand our world. A rapidly growing global population, limited resources, disruptive technology, and exponential change have created the perfect storm for confusion, fear, and unrest.

- *Education.* We've drifted away from civics education, and one could question if how we have collectively approached civics education has been effective.

- *The American system of government.* We're seeing polarization in the parliamentary system, but has our two-party system created more of a team mentality than is normal? Have lobbies undermined our rights as citizens? Has the American system become too dysfunctional to limit polarization?

- *Rise of nationalism.* The rise of nationalism is a byproduct of polarization and not the other way around. But once it is established—and it certainly has made an unfortunate comeback on the world stage—it breeds more of the polarization that created it.

We have more questions than answers and do not pretend to be experts in the underlying causes. Understanding some of these issues has helped us form our skillbuilders, but we realize how complicated and interconnected these issues are and know there is no simple solution to fixing these issues. We are interested in cleaning up the mess, not blaming someone for creating it. This is where we are right now, and we can each do our small part to contribute toward the solution.

OVERCOMING PUSHBACK

Let's address the obvious problem. Many people view teaching or learning civics as admirable but view being political as toxic. But it's okay to be political. In fact, in case you haven't been reading the news, the world is at a pivotal point. We need you to be political. Depending on the country you live in (especially the US), some of these ideas might make you uncomfortable. However, that only proves just how much we need these conversations and deep reflections.

Before we begin this book, let's take a moment to reflect on what "*civics*" means and remind ourselves about how politics is an inevitable byproduct of civics. We say this because we need politics to be embraced and endeared, not loathed and avoided because we want to avoid problems. By avoiding political discourse (and other tough topics) altogether, we end up with stagnation and dysfunction.

In the US, we often believe middle and high school civics or government classes are important to build awareness for our students to be responsible members of our representative democracy. As we just mentioned, civics is the study of the rights and duties of citizenship, and on the surface, few would challenge the merit of introducing these concepts to our young people. If you scratch deeper, however, you will see that learning about issues in civics quickly leads to views of negativity, controversy, or disdain.

Teaching civics has become delicate for many educators. There are teachers who are concerned about how people might misconstrue their lessons. There are those who might even find themselves in potential trouble with administration or school board members if their lessons don't align with the mentality of the district for which they work. This has nothing to do with civics. It has everything to do with politics. Our society's dysfunctional political existence has created a toxic vibe in American classrooms that paves the way for student disdain of the subject and disdain for politics.

But when we step back and analyze what *politics* truly means, it's clear that we are missing the mark in sending an understanding of this meaning to our students. So, what exactly is politics? The Greek origin of the word simply translates to "dealing with issues of the city." When assessing the relationship between civics and politics, one might say that politics is the soul to the body of civics in the same way that spirituality plays a role in religion. Thinking of it in this way should bring about thoughts of community, personal responsibility, and a need to work together.

Is that how we view issues related to politics today? Has the root of the word lost its relevance to today? It is certainly easy to cynically think that indeed it has. Today, people view politics as associated with painful views. We tend to emphasize the conflicts in politics, and we are often socialized to either turn away completely (be non-confrontational) or view politics only as a combative subject (be confrontational). It is as though we have established only two lanes to deal with politics, and neither provides a path for a functional democracy. Undoubtedly, this dysfunction has negatively impacted how our young people typically view politics today.

In our quest to answer why we've become so divided, why having a civics education isn't enough, we've found that it's because our society has a negative view of being political. We need being political to be associated with something positive. We need the term "political" to be associated with kindness, intelligence, and forward thinking. Too many people remain silent while the attention goes to simplistic and bold people who often are free of the desire to broaden their understanding of issues and therefore only ratchet up the polarization.

Politics needs to be introduced to students as a concept that is relevant to them and is associated with topics they care about. It needs to be meshed into our curriculums well beyond the civics classroom and viewed as part of our way of life.

We are socialized in the US to avoid discussing politics. We're scared that if teachers bring up tough topics, we're indoctrinating students, or if teachers don't like the viewpoints of students, they'll grade them poorly. This is not what excellent teachers do, and we can't let this viewpoint prevent us from teaching critical thought or prohibit our students from meaningfully engaging in civics.

This is a big reason that we don't know how to have discourse, and we see people fall into the two categories of either being politically non-confrontational or politically confrontational. Teaching civic-mindedness works to fight this. We should embrace talking about politics. We should teach effective methods to do so. Discourse should advocate in these broad ways, as we will see in this book. All teachers need to help nurture this mindset, just as they do with issues like promoting good health decisions and using kindness to fight bullying.

Do not be afraid to get political. It's the only way to teach our students to do the same. And if that notion makes you uncomfortable, it further exemplifies just how inaccurate we've become in providing a proper civics education. If you're having doubts or feeling nervous, we want to settle those nerves. We know you might face resistance (sometimes even from yourself), but if not you, then who? We need you to help drive this work. It's critical that we, as teachers, don't fall into the trap of inactivity. With all this said, here are a few steps we can take and actions we can deploy in the face of pushback. Hopefully, these points will provide you with moral support and sound reasoning to use when communicating with the naysayers.

Don't let others make excuses to avoid difficult topics. Often, people make excuses for our students, saying it's their young age or inability to cope, but from what we see in a lot of adults, they've never learned to reflect on their thoughts, actions, and feelings when confronted with complicated issues. When life happens, the "just kids" excuse to avoid dealing with reality might often do more harm than good. It's okay to remind others that students could benefit from our guidance, and that's what we're here for.

Rethink assessments. As soon as the emphasis on learning is on content and not skills, it takes away some of the most valuable techniques we can use to teach the 4 Cs: *critical thinking, collaboration, creativity, and communication.* Whenever possible, explain why it is necessary to use assessments that help students improve their skills, as it's the skills that will improve students' abilities to work with others and engage in consensus-building.

Communicate with parents. It's important we communicate upfront with parents about our goals. We believe the message we need to send to parents is that this is not about aimlessly discussing controversy but rather instilling the ability for their child to have a voice, communicate with others, and ultimately emerge into a critical thinker. Critical thinking is a skill built from taking in various viewpoints and sources of information and making an informed decision to the best of your ability. Here is a sample message that educators can continually promote to hesitant parents:

> *The more we censor and shelter our children, the less they can develop this skill. Censoring does not mean protecting our children; we're preventing them from being critically thinking adults. We must let them practice like they'll play.*

Be patient as students work through their biases. Remember, all students are learners. They're questioning what their parents, religions, peers, and the media have taught them. It is our job to help them navigate through and come up with the answers on their own. This means that you cannot discriminate against students based on what they believe. Our job is not to get students to believe what you believe but to build the critical skills necessary for them to think for themselves. Don't be surprised if it takes months—or the whole school year—to see their growth.

Don't feel pressured by the constraints of compliance. Many are weary of even the idea of going against the preferred or mandated expectations, whether locally or at the state level. Ultimately, we need to do what we know to be right. We have found that our colleagues can help provide the courage we need to resist the urge to comply, to just keep our heads down and get through the day, even when we know we should take a stand. Communicate with each other openly.

As we head into the ten chapters, we ask that you keep these points in the back of your mind. Making real change for the better isn't easy. Being clear-eyed about knowing what we are up against is critical. But we must move in the right direction for the next generation. So without further ado, let's dig in and get started.

CHAPTER I

PRACTICE SENSE-MAKING

Equip students with strategies to question the world and their roles in it

Don't just tell your children about the world, show them.
– UNKNOWN

> **Essential Question:** How do you help students understand the world and their roles in it?
>
> **Objective:** If we want to help students discover what they care about and to find their purpose, we must do more to help them make sense of the world. It's hard to know what problems to solve or the role you might play if you've never been given an opportunity to question the world and how it works.

THE PROBLEM: WE AVOID LETTING CHILDREN EXPERIENCE THE WORLD FOR THEMSELVES

L ET'S SAY YOU are at the store and overhear a child talking to their mother. "Mom, can I have that toy?" The mother swiftly responds, "If you use your own money."

The child looks to be about five, and you can see the confused look on their face. "But I don't have any money. Where do I get money from? Can't you just use your credit card? That always works."

The mother responds, "Maybe later, honey," and they drop the issue as they go about their way, leaving the child as unaware as they were before. Imagine, however, if the mother took that opportunity to explain some basics about finances to her child. She might have shown the price tag to the child so they could understand how much money it would cost to purchase the item. She might have said that she receives money from working and asked if there were any ways her daughter thought she might be able to earn money (chores or a lemonade stand). At the cash register, she might have had her daughter hold the money and give it to the clerk so the child could experience the transaction that comes from exchanging cash for goods and services. It would be through this sense-making that the child would start to formulate her understanding of how money works.

Children want to know and understand how the world works. Sometimes their questions feel too deep or advanced for their age, so we may avoid them or decide to shield them from reality. What's the harm, right? But we're preventing our youth from being the independent critical thinkers we so desperately need. If they are old enough to ask, they are usually old enough to know or at least to be taken seriously. As high school teachers, we have noticed an alarming number of students who still do not understand where money comes from, but they know their parent's credit card seems to have an endless supply. Maybe they needed that conversation in the early years after all.

Sometimes we push children to answer questions they're not asking themselves yet. The classic question, "What do you want to be when you grow up?" comes to mind, as it's one we've probably all been asked at some point. It's a question so commonplace that you might have posed it to your children or students.

While this question seems innocent, it captures the very essence of our first chapter—*sense-making*. How could we expect a child with a limited (or should we say, idealistic) view of how the world works to determine the role they will play, the job they will do in twenty years' time? It makes us wonder why we're so apt to ask this question prematurely, especially in a world that is rapidly changing. A foundation would be to encourage our youth to make sense of the world little by little so they can understand how fluid it is and how their world and their place in it might change.

> *Kids need to experience the world for themselves, rather than hear us tell them how we think they should experience it.*

Adam Grant wrote an article that challenged readers to stop asking children what they wanted to be when they grew up and instead suggested asking young people the type of person they want to be, or the problems they wanted to solve. It's interesting how a slight shift in focus can make a world of difference in what we consider important and where we invest our energy. It also provides parameters to help children make sense of why they do things and gain a better understanding of their motivations and the contributions they have the potential to make.

THE SOLUTION: PRACTICE SENSE-MAKING

Sense-making can equip our students with a process to help them navigate the world. We cannot expect students to solve local or global challenges if they cannot grasp what those challenges might be. Do we want students going through the motions just to get a job, or do we want students to find fulfillment and purpose through their life and work? If we want civic-minded adults, ready to tackle the challenges of tomorrow, the first step is to give space for exploration, to make connections as to how things work, and to understand that situations often change.

In most current educational models, we get pushed into a lifestyle, into a routine, into norms we might not strive for if left to our own devices. Too often, and it starts from a young age, we define ourselves not by our own terms but by society's terms. We might not be encouraged to question or gain a deeper understanding of why things are the way they are. We often do what we think our parents want, what our teachers want, and what our peers want, without pushing ourselves to think deeply about why we do the things we do. Do our actions align with our values? Are we investing our time and energy into what brings meaning into our lives and the lives of others?

Are we truly encouraging students to think about the type of person they want to be? Are we challenging them to think deeply about the type of life they want to lead? Are we answering the questions they are asking us, regardless of whether we feel they're age-appropriate? Kids need to experience the world for themselves, rather than hear us tell them how we think they should experience it.

School should be a place of discovery, and while academics remain the focus, ample opportunities exist for students to learn more about themselves—their skills, talents, interests, experiences, and passions—by providing them with opportunities to make sense of their world and how they fit into it. In this way, they can find their purpose. We cannot expect students to change the world when they haven't yet discovered how things work. Providing them with outlets to pursue the topics they care about (or that bother them)—and exposing them to new challenges they might not have known before—would put them on the right path toward discovering how they might make their mark on the world.

As adults, we have two options. One is to encourage students to do what has always been done, and the other is to work to build the type of future we want to leave behind. As Socrates said, "The secret of change is to focus all your energy, not on fighting the old, but on building the new." Sense-making is the key to equipping our youth with an understanding of the world that can help them adapt and tackle complex problems.

Polarization happens in times of rapid change. Some people want to cling to what they know, and others are ready to embrace needed changes to build the future. This polarization gets compounded when we focus on the superficial (for example, high gas prices) without attempting to dig deeper into the problem. When we don't understand the overall situation or think deeply about our purpose, our planet, or where we stand, it's easy to get manipulated or to fight for what doesn't matter.

"Bumper sticker" politics (for example, Governor "So and So" Sucks) is a great example of this polarization. In addition, when we don't understand our purpose or value, we lose sight of how much each one of us matters and how much our individual actions matter. Groupthink can have incredibly detrimental effects and is a driver of polarization. We'll discuss more about these skills later but wanted to highlight here why sense-making can help ground us so we don't develop a contrived notion of who we are and what we stand for.

CIVICS CONNECTION: SENSE-MAKING IS ONE OF THE MOST FUNDAMENTAL SKILLS A CHILD CAN LEARN

As we discussed in the Introduction, civics classes often focus too much on teaching the most important aspects of how a government works. We cover how government functions, its bodies, and the moving parts needed to turn ideas into law. When you describe how a government functions without ever getting into its true purpose and impact, it can feel incredibly abstract and irrelevant, especially to a student.

Students need sense-making to truly grasp the power of policy, how decisions and leaders shape our systems, and how these systems impact our daily lives. We can use civics class as a forum to discuss relevant issues so students can make connections and better understand how things work. For many students, it's their first experience diving into the complexities of issues such as healthcare, education, trade, international relations, taxes, environment, equity, food security, energy security, and gun rights.

Students are limited when they are not encouraged to question their world. One of the largest barriers to discussing issues comes when students have already labeled themselves as belonging to a certain political party based on misperceptions. These misperceptions often come from students being told how the world works instead of being provided with an opportunity to uncover and discover this for themselves. This problem becomes even more complicated when people support political candidates based on their identity and no longer investigate the policies being implemented by their party.

The lack of sense-making, coupled with an imposed cultural identity, drives polarization. Once an affiliation with a party becomes cultural, a tradition passed on from generation to generation, it becomes harder to have meaningful discussions because questioning the party (or its policies) becomes personal and, consequently, emotionally and inevitably divisive.

To find the thread that unites us, we need to encourage more sense-making. Allowing students to focus on issues and explore policies prevents polarization because it enables them to practice making connections and to understand the consequences that various decisions might bring. This lens enables us to work with young people one idea at a time and helps us compartmentalize so people can differentiate between their assumed identity and the problem at hand. By forming an opinion on policies, students can uncover more about themselves, their values, and what's important to them. From there, we can use the civics classroom to help students connect the dots as to how their values and their vision of the world equate to policy. Inevitably, these connections are more likely to build consensus than divide and polarize us.

Sense-making facilitates introspection and encourages us to entertain ideas as we try to understand issues. The more students do this, the more they uncover where and how they can do their part, what problems they gravitate toward, their purpose, and the contributions they can make to the world. It is critical for students to have a voice and opinion on the issues that will shape their world, and it's up to us to help them think deeply and holistically about their roles.

Our goal as civics teachers is to help students understand that the actions of government will directly impact their lives, and that's why they need to get involved. That's the real reason they learn civics. In the reality of real-world government, good policy, good leadership, and good systems create the greatest impact. Data-driven policies have proven effectiveness in issues such as tax reform, renewable energy, education reform, and health issues because real data provides objectivity for the need and rationale to create these policies.

For example, we have seen marked improvements in policies in many Western US states since initiatives have become more prevalent and require data and science to drive policy implementation. As reported in a *U.S. News & World Report* article by journalist Casey Leins, Colorado launched the Governor's Dashboard in 2019, a website that outlines four key issues to address: tax reform and economic development, energy and renewables, education and the workforce, and health. The state's goals, along with charts tracking how close Colorado is to achieving those goals, are visible for web users to see. In short, policy is being driven by transparent data.

These efforts consequently trickle down into motivating politicians to lead under these principles, which, in effect, strengthens the overall structure of government even more. And it's not just occurring in the United States. We see this playing out in governments throughout western Europe as well.

Wrapping back around to the classroom environment, the more students discover on their own, the more likely they are to contribute to the type of world they want to live in by supporting solid systemic changes. These changes bring about politicians who demonstrate their leadership by being policy-oriented. The hopeful result is that our students are more likely to get active in politics and understand the value of being a part of it, not just see the relevance of what they learn in civics.

This is where teachers of all subjects and areas can make a difference. All educators at all levels can play a key role in helping students practice sense-making so they recognize what they care about. Then, when they eventually get to civics class, they're better equipped to understand how politics connects to the issues they have a vested interest in.

MAKE THIS SKILL A REALITY

The world has many problems, and we need to equip students to solve them. But it's not as easy as it sounds. As educators, we know it's part of our job to encourage critical, independent thinkers, but students are not always ready to question the world. We want to challenge them to form opinions and to have a solid understanding of themselves, but it often feels like an uphill battle. For instance:

- You ask for their opinion, and they don't have one.

- You try to provide choice, and they stare at you with open mouths.

- You try to ask questions, and only one or two respond.

- You try passion projects—and it turns out they're not passionate about anything.

For us, sense-making is part of a key piece of problem-solving, but it can also create a dilemma. If you don't understand your world, you may not be aware of any problems to solve. If you don't have any problems to solve, why would you engage in sense-making? But ignorance is not so blissful after all when you realize that decisions and policies impact you negatively, and you didn't even try to have a say. We believe sense-making happens in the classroom by helping students notice the world around them. We can do this by asking open-ended questions and by presenting them with problems and letting them toy around and tinker with ideas.

STRATEGIES YOU CAN IMPLEMENT RIGHT AWAY

Idea #1: Ask more *why* and *how* questions.

While there are no bad questions, how you ask generates different responses. Sometimes it's necessary to experiment with what works. One way to ensure we're asking more exploratory questions is to reframe *what* questions with *why* or *how*. These types of questions often encourage us to synthesize information, make connections, and dig deeper into what we are learning.

For instance, if you ask students, "What makes plants grow?" you might get responses such as soil, sunlight, and water. However, when you ask, "*How* do plants grow?" you will often get a deeper answer with more synthesis. A student might respond with, "You plant a seed in the soil. It needs rainfall and sunlight to get bigger."

How are the questions you ask students facilitating more sense-making? (For more about using questions in the classroom, see the book *Hacking Questions* by Connie Hamilton.)

Idea #2: Allow time for tinker and play.

Allowing time for tinker and play within almost every lesson or activity is important for both sense-making and curiosity. People learn best when they are actively involved. We know that play engages students in learning, helps them make connections, and generates questions as they gain a deeper understanding. Teachers have countless ways to encourage students to engage with materials. We know STEM games, problem-based learning, and simulations help to facilitate experiences where students can apply their learning. While we hope teachers try to employ this type of pedagogy as often as possible, we recognize it's daunting to incorporate into every lesson.

We have a general rule of thumb that for every ten minutes of instruction, we try to include five minutes of play. Provide a space where students get to use their voice, practice their skills, and interact with the material. The questions start when students suddenly must use what they've learned.

Idea #3: Play the *How It Works* activity.

If you ask most people if they understand how their cell phone works, they might say yes. If you ask them for an actual explanation, they may struggle. Give students the opportunity to explore a topic and explain how it works. Have them take an ordinary item or activity and see if they can explain it.

- The produce in the grocery store. How did it get there? Explain how it works.

- A car. What allows it to run? Explain how it works.

- The television. How do programs get paid for? Explain how it works.

- The shower. How do you get hot running water? Explain how it works.

- The internet. What makes Google possible? Explain how it works.

- Choose your own and explain how it works.

Idea #4: Let students figure it out.

Ditch the directions. If possible, give students an assignment with an end goal but minimal guidance as to how they achieve that goal. Create a single prompt that would force them to apply content as they see fit. See what they can do on their own.

Examples:

- Create an event agenda for world leaders to discuss food security.

- Create a video that inspires others to take care of their mental health.

- Pitch an idea to the principal to engage students in healthy eating.

- Make a test for your peers using _____ content (for example, notes from Chapter 5).

- Design a prototype for an app that helps students with their writing.

Idea #5: Play the *Pack Your Suitcase* activity.

Have students pick a destination they would like to go to, then tell them they need to pack a suitcase for their trip. Have them write down all the items they would pack so they have a successful journey. Afterward, ask them to explain to a partner why they picked what they did. How did their experiences guide them to determine the items they would need? For those with similar destinations, did they pick similar items for their suitcases?

Relate this back to sense-making. How do our experiences help us make sense of our world and how we act in it?

CHAPTER 2

KEEP ASKING QUESTIONS

Keep curiosity alive for critical and deep thinking

One thing I know is I know nothing.
– SOCRATES

> **Essential Question:** How do we keep curiosity alive and encourage students to be skeptical?
>
> **Objective:** Help students broaden their understanding of concepts and information they learn by providing skills to strengthen and deepen their critical thinking.

THE PROBLEM: AS WE AGE, WE LOSE OUR SENSE OF CURIOSITY, WHICH CLOSES OUR MINDS

I, MICHELLE, REMEMBER talking with my children about the snow falling outside. As an adult seeing snow, my thoughts went to the obvious and practical, flipping between my appreciation for its beauty and a quick calculation of when I should start shoveling. To my daughters, however, a whole new magical world was falling beyond the window. They asked, "What is snow? How is it made? Is it snowing in China now, too?" Their curiosity was pushing them to a new level of depth on the subject, a curiosity I had somehow lost a long time ago.

Younger children are experts in questioning and are rarely satisfied with superficial answers. Virtually every young child on this planet is on a quest to understand the world around them. Their openness and thirst for knowledge are exemplary. These qualities are also the keys to promoting critical thinking and sensemaking. Once you stop asking questions, once you feel you have it all figured out, and once you're complacent—your curiosity dies. Without curiosity, you've lost your path toward thinking deeply and critically about the world around you.

Natural curiosity is a key ingredient to true learning and understanding. But as we get older, that reflective tendency to question dissipates. We accept our routine life as the status quo and the world we know and live in as the absolute. We stop asking why, how, or what if. We lose our sense-making abilities. Given the complexity of the world and the rapid change we experience, it's unhealthy to lose our sense of wonder or our skepticism. Accepting what we know on a surface level and never going deeper can be detrimental to our livelihood, our workplace, our relationships, and the policies we create (or dismantle). It can cause us to stay stuck in place as the world rapidly moves forward or, as the expression goes, to be so far behind we think we are first.

The problem of a lack of curiosity takes on a new level of severity when it becomes unacceptable to question the cultural and political elements of our world. Our egos might tell us we have nothing more to learn. When we stop asking questions, we can become set in our ways. We might only surround ourselves with people who think like us and validate our ideas.

Polarization occurs when we make it unacceptable to ask questions. When we can no longer entertain new ideas, our minds narrow. And when we confuse asking questions with taking sides, we step into dangerous territory. Suddenly, we may dismiss or attack the questions of others because we cannot accept that entertaining an idea is part of critical thought. It doesn't mean you have to agree with or accept the idea, but you should at least consider it.

We become resistant to change when it becomes unacceptable to let our minds explore, and communication breaks down when we refuse to let others ask why. Curiosity—asking questions—is a critical ingredient in sparking new ideas, testing our assumptions, and thinking beyond what we already know. It's an essential component for making progress toward understanding the complex layers that often exist with many societal issues.

It makes us wonder what might happen if more adults continued to question the world. For example, no one cares more about their lawns than Americans. According to studies at Baylor University, as of 2015, the United States was spending around $76 billion on lawn care annually, with second place going to Australia at $3 billion. Americans love a nicely manicured lawn; it's in the culture to mow. But why do people mow? What purpose does it truly serve? As an American, it's normal not to question why we mow but to just do it. Everyone else does it, and America's been mowing for years. It's just the way it is, and for many, it's the way it should be.

But what happens when we take a deeper look? What happens when we question?

We mention mowing for an interesting reason. It's a habit that seems harmless, but when done en masse can have profound impacts. Mowing actually has a tremendous impact on our environment. Mowing decreases biodiversity, and a loss of natural ecosystems results in fewer pollinators. A decline in pollinators can lead to repercussions in food security. In recent years, it's become more common for states to create no-mow zones along highways. It not only has saved millions of dollars for these states in lawn care costs, but it also has brought back natural vegetation (such as milkweed) that is critical to the survival of bees and butterflies.

Their livelihood is vital for our food security, not to mention that tall grasses and wildflowers have sprung up from the medians, and they provide a different form of beauty compared to the manicured lawns they've replaced.

THE SOLUTION: KEEP ASKING QUESTIONS

This example of repercussions goes back to curiosity. As an American, if I question the need to mow, I know I'll receive a dismissive wave of the hand and be treated as if I'm ridiculous. People might become defensive when I ask my hypothetical question of what might happen if we mowed less. My mental exploration might be confused as a personal attack because most people mow their lawns, and they take offense at those who don't. Of course, this is not the aim of asking questions. Our curiosity helps us understand how things work and helps us grow mentally. When we reach the point where people meet our questions with hostility, then it's a sign they've lost their curiosity.

Questions can lead to change. With mowing, we are investing a lot of time and money in destroying some of the very habitats we need to thrive. Questions and curiosity can lead to deeper learning and understanding, which can lead to deeper dialogue and investigation, which can lead to positive change. The art of having discussions sparked by curiosity and questioning has helped evolve other practices around issues such as smoking cigarettes, littering, and consuming single-use plastics. When we entertain questions, it helps us discover new ideas. From there, we can form deep and critical thoughts on these subjects, and when enough people agree that the harm outweighs the good, we achieve positive results.

Isn't it incredible what happens when we pause and ask why? Even the most mundane task deserves a little curiosity, a little skepticism, because it might create an unintended impact. This leads us to wonder how we can keep curiosity alive as we age—both for our students and ourselves. How do we prevent our students from becoming the narrow-minded adults we've all encountered?

We all start out extremely inquisitive, but we need to nurture this innate ability, as we can quickly lose our edge. Research suggests that part of the reason lies within the classroom. A study conducted by the University of Michigan CS Mott Children's Hospital and the Center for Human Growth and Development, as reported in a 2020 article in *The Guardian*, found evidence that students consistently ask fewer questions in classroom environments as they get older. Middle school students ask fewer questions than primary students, and high school students ask fewer questions than middle school students.

This study also found evidence that classrooms where more student-led questions and curiosity emerge are driven by the teacher. The study's lead researcher, Dr. Prachi Shah, says, "Promoting curiosity in children, especially those from environments of economic disadvantage, may be an important, under-recognized way to address the achievement gap. Promoting curiosity is a foundation for early learning that we should emphasize more when we look at academic achievement."

As teachers and as parents, we have a tremendous opportunity—and responsibility—to nurture the curiosity of our youth. It's their curiosity that helps them adapt and evolve to changes in life and in the world. With this in mind, this section is about providing strategies to nurture that inquisitive nature in our students so it doesn't wane as they grow into adulthood. We want our youth to be lifelong learners who strive to truly understand and ask questions about the world around them. The ability to remain curious and skeptical, to always ask questions, is a key ingredient of the critical and deep thinking that we, as educators, strive to embed in our students to help them be successful into adulthood.

CIVICS CONNECTION: CURIOSITY HELPS PREVENT POLARIZATION

The need for curiosity and questioning is obviously relevant to all subjects, but even more so in civics. Asking questions is the only way to induce critical thinking in the civics classroom. It's concerning when we have students who aren't as curious or who just don't have questions.

In the civics classroom, we've run into an interesting conundrum. We often have students who, at the ripe age of thirteen to sixteen, think they fully know and understand the world. They don't have many questions because they believe they already have it all sorted out. On the other end of the spectrum, we have students who expect to be told what to think, not recognizing the relevance of the subject. They come in ready to have a correct answer from the textbook or from their notes. It would be ideal if those students showed up curious instead.

The civics classroom should be a place of questions, a space for never-ending dialogue where students explore issues and entertain ideas on how we might address those issues. It is a chance to make sense of how the government works and to develop strategies to find consensus among those we don't agree with. Governments are "living" entities, and we must treat them as such. Policies and politics will forever need to adapt and evolve with changing times, and students should end their civics education knowing the work will never be done. They need to continue to question and understand their world throughout their lifetime if they are to be engaged citizens.

Helping students develop curiosity by asking more questions might be one of the easiest activities to implement for any teacher.

Curiosity is a key ingredient in preventing polarization. Civics and politics come with ambiguity, and students need to know that ambiguity is acceptable, even necessary at times. We need to set students up to solve problems, and this requires the ability to stay curious and ask questions so they know how to investigate issues and make informed conclusions. Students need to understand that, when it comes to policies, you sometimes must make hard choices, and it can feel uncomfortable. You may have to reduce some criteria to what helps the most or harms the least. Ethics often come into play, and often there is more than one acceptable solution. We may have multiple issues to address at once.

For example, COVID-19 was presented as a choice between our safety and the economy, but why not ask how we could remain safe while also protecting the economy? Sometimes we might have good ideas, but we implement them poorly. Identify if it's the idea or the implementation that needs work. All of these require questioning and curiosity. They require a desire to know more and to seek the best solution possible.

Finally, curiosity helps students understand the relevance and impact a policy has on their lives. Understanding civics and getting an introduction to politics is an ideal setting for students to question and uncover more about their community, their country, and their world. As civics teachers, it's our duty to allow students to entertain a dialogue civilly as we work to answer those questions surrounding the policies and politics that impact them.

This questioning, this healthy dose of skepticism, is the key to sparking their quest for knowledge. From there, we can help students dig deeper and properly investigate their questions. This activates their need to look for sources and expertise so they can better understand their world, and it helps them ask better questions to identify which sources and experts are the most valid. Our goal is to encourage students to question everyone and everything so they can strengthen their critical thinking skills as adults. When presented with serious issues and additional sources, students who have the ability to ask better questions can create more informed conclusions. Students are our future voters, leaders, and policymakers. It's essential that their thirst for knowledge and understanding stays with them for life.

MAKE THIS SKILL A REALITY

Curiosity is the quest for knowledge. Questions keep us open-minded and are important to learning. The more we practice, the easier it becomes to ask better questions and work through problems. We become equipped to navigate our world, find information, and draw conclusions. It makes us more competent in identifying credible sources and determining the lines between fact and fiction. Questions make learning active and essential for us to gain a deeper sense of knowledge about any subject.

Adults ask significantly fewer questions than children, which leads us to conclude that we're becoming less curious and less open-minded as we age. But why? Helping students develop curiosity by asking more questions might be one of the easiest activities to implement for any teacher. We can be more intentional in nurturing our students' curiosity by changing how we assess and how we use class time. Do we demand our students ask questions? Do we provide students with time to explore or to let their minds wander? When asked questions, are we patient and thoughtful?

STRATEGIES YOU CAN IMPLEMENT RIGHT AWAY

Idea #6: Play the *Dig for Water* game.

This is a game in which students generate new questions by building on other questions. To play:

- Put your students in groups of around three kids. Explain that they will each have a turn to develop a question based on another student's question. The only rule is that the questions they create should tie into the content.

- Give them a starting question. Example: "Why did World War I start?"

- The first student will apply knowledge to develop a follow-up question: "Why was there an arms race?" And then the third student asks a question, and the game continues.

- Try to reach a total of ten questions.

Idea #7: Play *Question Quota*.

Perhaps it's not that students don't have questions but they need us to be more intentional in asking them what questions they have. Encourage students to write down a certain number of questions on a topic or assignment using a Question Quota. This ensures we're helping students keep the questions coming, and hopefully, they begin generating a healthy habit.

See Image 2.1 for a few ideas to incorporate a Question Quota into daily classroom activities.

IDEAS TO INCORPORATE A QUESTION QUOTA INTO DAILY CLASSROOM ACTIVITIES

Exit Ticket Questions	Weekly Quotas	Assignment Questions
Request that students submit three questions they still have (even if they're random) after a lesson. (Helpful teacher tip: Avoid asking, "Do you have any questions?" This invites students to say no.)	Ask students to keep a question journal and submit twenty questions that popped in their head that week. Try to do the same for yourself. Not only does it help with understanding, but it also enables us to reflect on the work we are doing.	Encourage students to write at least one question they have about an assignment on their actual assignment. It's okay for them to write down whatever popped in their head as they were working on it.

Image 2.1

Idea #8: Take on real-world questions.

Sometimes, with the best of intentions, we have a natural tendency to shield our students from the world. They often have important questions about why things are the way they are or how the world works. They may have no one to ask, which is why they come to us. How are you creating opportunities to help them navigate the world they are experiencing?

Consider these ideas about student questions:

- *It's often relevant to them.* We know student questions might not always be relevant to the content, but the questions could be related to how they're feeling or how they're experiencing the world. If they ask, they're looking for guidance, so it's important that we take their questions seriously.

- *Create an outlet for questions.* It's understandable if you can't always use class time to help students work through their questions. Is there another way they can communicate with you? Do students have a private or anonymous way they could reach out? Can they meet you over their lunch break? Do you use journals or another outlet for students to navigate what they are experiencing?

- *You don't need to give them answers.* Many students aren't looking to be told an actual answer to their questions. They just need someone to bounce around ideas with as their minds make connections. We can become a needed ear by having these discussions as they push their thinking.

Idea #9: Observe your world.

We've all had a commute (car ride, bus ride, or walk) that we've done for so long that we're on autopilot. We may stop noticing our surroundings, and someone else pointing out a change can surprise us. We pass a certain spot every day and never pay attention to it. It's important that we learn to keep observing our world like a five-year-old. It's why they have so many questions and learn so quickly.

Encourage your students to get used to observing their world and asking questions, especially outside of the classroom. Give prompts that encourage them to keep their eyes and ears open, and have them write down a few questions from their observation.

Example prompts for your students:

- Go outside for fifteen minutes. *What did you notice? What questions did it generate?*

- Pay attention to your route while on your way to school. *Did you notice anything you hadn't noticed before? What questions does it prompt?*

- Notice the interactions of your family as you ate dinner. *What did you learn? What questions do you have?*

- Observe the lunchroom. *What does it tell you about your peers? What questions came to mind?*

Idea #10: Up your brainstorming game.

Sometimes when we want students to brainstorm ideas, we might just say, "Brainstorm," and leave it at that. When students feel stuck or uncreative, you can inspire them to ask more questions and generate more ideas. For example, IDEO U provides a wide range of activities that support students with ideation on their Brainstorming Resources page. Here are a few we recommend:

- **Mash-up.** Bring unexpected items together to spark inspiration. For example, how might aliens view our planet? How might a four-year-old rule as president?

- **Silent brainstorming.** Avoid groupthink by giving students the opportunity to each think about their own ideas before working together. Prior to a group conversation, ask them to write ideas on sticky notes or a sheet of paper before combining their ideas.

- **Constraints.** Add limitations to a challenge to push thinking. For example, how might we share information without the internet? How might we commute if we were to get rid of cars?

- **Other people's shoes.** Encourage students to imagine what a challenge is like for a different person. Have them storyboard or role-play. How might a five-year-old approach this challenge? A seventy-year-old?

CHAPTER 3

CULTIVATE HUMILITY

Prevent ego from breaking down dialogue

Pride is concerned with who is right. Humility is concerned with what is right.

— EZRA TAFT BENSON

> **Essential Question:** How do we help students to be open to new ideas? How do we help students manage their egos so they might always strive for growth in their learning and understanding?
>
> **Objective:** Help students learn strategies to keep their egos in check so they might keep an open mind, be okay with being wrong, learn from mistakes, and know that these experiences are the key building blocks to how we learn and grow.

THE PROBLEM: OUR EGO IMPEDES LEARNING

REFLECT ON THIS scenario for a moment: Out of the blue, a friend or loved one sends you a video they want you to watch, but it's about a topic you quickly debunk. Even though a quick Google search can validate that this is misinformation, the sender doesn't want to hear it. You wonder why they will not accept that what they've sent is false. Why won't they listen? Why won't they accept valid sources that clearly disprove the misinformation they've sent?

Then it hits you. They didn't send it to you to have a conversation; they sent it to validate their beliefs, to convince you of their worldview, no matter how flawed it might be.

Our first reaction might be to get angry. It might be to shame the other person because you can't believe how "stupid" they are. But shaming and anger don't work. In fact, they may just exacerbate the situation. Often, in these circumstances, we are dealing with someone else's ego. Perhaps they have low self-esteem and are attempting to overcompensate. For them, it's not so much about the issue but about feeling unique or more knowledgeable. They want to look smart.

As we mentioned in the Introduction, the Dunning-Kruger effect is a studied phenomenon in which people who lack skills or knowledge in a certain area overestimate their abilities. It's difficult to have a conversation with them because they are not concerned about learning or the issue itself. They have their ego wrapped up in whatever argument they are trying to make.

As discouraging as this may be, when we recognize that there may be some deeper psychological issues at play, it can help us be more understanding. This is where humility might offer all of us a bit of respite. When we take a step back to assess the situation, to check our egos, we can have far better results. If you want people to keep an open mind, to base their conclusions on fact and reason and not emotion and assumption, you must model the same. Sometimes—and we know it can be a painful experience— you have to be willing to entertain new ideas, no matter how silly they may seem, if you want to open up a dialogue.

THE SOLUTION: CULTIVATE HUMILITY

This is where the art of humility can support us. If we take a moment to reflect on the situation, it can help us put our egos aside and better deal with the situation. Consider whether you are arguing to be right or if a bigger goal was in mind. If it's the latter, if the video was spreading something discriminatory, then it is worthwhile to continue the conversation. One step to keep our ego in check is to keep the end goal or big picture in mind as we discuss issues to ensure we're not just arguing for the sake of being right.

When individuals learn to properly discuss issues, they recognize that sharing information, exchanging ideas, asking questions, and disagreeing on certain points are normal parts of learning and compromising.

A second step in practicing humility is simply to listen to others and remember that you might have more to learn as well. You might be under the false impression that you know more than you actually do. It's best to hear others out, as you never know what insights you might gain. In addition, those with low self-esteem may just need validation, and the simple act of listening to them, regardless of how absurd you feel their ideas are, is enough to show a level of respect and dignity so they put their defenses down and become open to dialogue.

A third step in practicing humility may be to manage our emotions. Often, it's hard to monitor our reactions. Recognizing our weaknesses can help us employ better communication techniques so we might meet people where they are without leaving them feeling belittled or embarrassed. As educators, it's often easier to do this with students because we know they are young people who are learning. But adults may need the same type of nurturing. We live in a world where social media makes it easy to find content in the media to justify our emotions, assumptions, and beliefs, so many people become closed to new ideas.

Once they reach a point where they believe they are entitled to their opinion, no matter how little substance it has, that person might be out of reach. Instead of always being reactive, we may need to walk away. We cannot change everyone's mind on everything, nor should we. It's up to us to figure out which issues and goals are important and to best invest our time and energy into initiatives that can create an impact.

As educators, we don't want ego-driven dialogue to prevent our students from having the constructive conversations they so desperately need to build consensus and solve problems. Practicing humility and managing egos are key strategies to help us cultivate open minds. When individuals learn to properly discuss issues, they recognize that sharing information, exchanging ideas, asking questions, and disagreeing on certain points are normal parts of learning and compromising. When our egos become too involved, issues suddenly become too personal. We may not be open to investigating our bias or searching for knowledge because the fear of being wrong is too great of a risk to our self-image.

In a world that is rapidly changing, we need to trust one another and remember that no one can know everything. We are each just a small piece of this thing called humanity. Humility can help us remember that. We have experts in every field out there, and we often must rely on one another and appreciate others' knowledge. Disruptions in technology, advances in science, and changes in society require us to seek new information and new ways of doing things. We cannot let our egos impede solving problems and making the world better.

CIVICS CONNECTION: HUMILITY OPENS THE DOOR TO FINDING THE TRUTH

In the civics classroom, conversations can potentially quickly turn into "I'm right, you're wrong" tirades that are counterproductive to dialogue. Political parties might feel more like sports teams. While it may be taboo to talk about politics in public, people certainly talk about them behind closed doors. Ugly truths come out, and students, who rarely know any better, are exposed and impressionable as to what they hear outside of the classroom. Facts and science in some situations may become controversial because suddenly, students must face a new reality in which what they believe is true might not mesh with factual reality. This is when ego and identity can hinder learning. Students can confuse questioning and debate as attacks on their way of life, their loved ones, and themselves. They may be resistant to listening to others or accepting facts.

For these reasons, it's become commonplace to avoid conversations to spare feelings and moments of discomfort. All this does is protect our egos at the high price of forgetting our goals. We need to clean the air of suspicion that teachers are trying to get students to join the other side. Conversations are not meant to prove others wrong but to take students on a learning journey where they can uncover new ideas for themselves. We should view the civics classroom as a playing field for students to respectfully learn the skills of critical thinking and communication. This means putting our egos aside, assuming good intentions, and giving one another a chance to be heard and express our views.

Humility would help us see we are in the same communities together and need to work together to solve the same problems. When an issue suddenly becomes so divisive (complicated issues are rarely binary) that we feel we must take sides, we stop looking for common ground, and polarization starts. When our egos tell us we already know everything and there is nothing left to learn, or that anyone who proposes an alternative idea is engaging in a personal attack, we have a problem. We each need to put our defenses down a bit more and welcome new ideas. This means meeting people where they are. It means being tolerant and patient with others. We are all at different starting points in our learning journeys for different topics, and shaming is one of the fastest ways to encourage someone to put their walls back up.

In an era where we are finding more students feeling a sense of hopelessness about the future, we need to provide them with strategies to act and make needed changes. The world does not need superheroes. We need collective leadership. When we empower our students to accept that we each have a humble but important role to play in working together, students can understand that it is how we make progress. We all have seen firsthand the damage that can be done when we make decisions based on ego, not on impact or outcomes.

If we don't model to students the importance of entertaining new ideas, then we will continue to build momentum for this "us versus them" polarized world that currently contributes to the polarization we experience. Eight billion people live on this planet. We have too much at stake not to learn to keep our egos in check so we might see the bigger picture and work together to find solutions. There is no way we will all agree on everything, and it's best to learn at a young age how to deal with the discomfort that inevitably comes from disagreeing or being wrong. In the political arena, it is essential that people can converse, play with new ideas (even ones they don't agree with), and respectfully disagree, and the classroom is an excellent place to equip students with those skills. As the world continues to turn, we will need to balance shaping its future while also addressing the problems at hand. This duality requires effective communication and being open to new ideas—and humility can help.

MAKE THIS SKILL A REALITY

We've all had students come to us with something outlandish they've learned at home. Perhaps a child comes in and argues she doesn't need to wash her hands with soap because her big brother told her that handwashing was only for kids with "cooties." Another student says you need to check your sources; the Earth is flat, and he knows that because his grandpa told him so. It can feel like an uphill battle to help students unlearn some things they've been taught, especially when finding out otherwise might crush their egos.

We are sure the civics classroom is not students' first experience having their egos tested. Learning is a journey, and the more we can do to equate learning to growth and not to ego, the better. In an education system that often forces us to assess in terms of wrong versus right, and rewards certain forms of intelligence over others, it can be difficult to ensure students don't feel "dumb" when they are learning new things. Often, it's how we deal with these issues that lays the groundwork for how students approach learning and how intertwined it becomes with their sense of self-worth. If we simply tell them they are wrong, then we don't empower them to find out the truth for themselves.

Fortunately, these instances also present us with opportunities to demonstrate the normalcy that comes from not knowing or from having to unlearn false facts. The sooner students recognize that it's okay to learn, unlearn, discover, make mistakes, take risks, and change their minds, the less they wrap their egos around being correct or better than others. The more students practice piquing their curiosity, the more likely they are to practice humility in the future.

For example, two plus two equals four, and there's no arguing with that. When a child gives us an incorrect answer, we can tell them it's wrong, or we can tell them to keep trying and help them uncover a strategy to get to the answer. This is true for anything we learn. To take that a step further, we can always reframe an idea so it offers students an opportunity for exploration.

For those students who come in with flat Earth theories, for example, we might provide them with information on early space endeavors and how and when the first photos of the earth were taken from space. We can then add stories of people who have trekked around the world heading in the same direction and returned to their original spot. We can respect students' experiences and safeguard their egos by teaching them to have an open mind. When students realize trial and error is all a part of the process, it can help them internalize that their sense of self-worth should not be wrapped up in knowing everything or getting everything right. This reality will certainly lead to the students developing more humility. When we are humble enough to know it is okay not to know everything, then we are on the right path.

The ego is tricky. We want confident kids, but we need to perform a balancing act to ensure we don't turn into overly confident adults. Below are a few ideas we developed to help you get your students to become more open to learning and embracing truth through due diligence.

STRATEGIES YOU CAN IMPLEMENT RIGHT AWAY

Idea #11: Normalize not knowing.

Teaching requires us to leave our egos at the door. The first step in cultivating open-mindedness is to model it ourselves. Students absorb everything we do, and since they might not see it at home, it becomes even more essential that we show what this looks like. If we model the behavior we'd like to see them exhibit, they may follow suit and practice open-mindedness too. See Image 3.1 for a few ideas on how to create open-mindedness in the classroom.

HOW TO CREATE OPEN-MINDEDNESS IN THE CLASSROOM

#1: Admit when you're wrong	Own when you don't know something. Make it acceptable to say, "I was wrong."
	Don't be embarrassed to correct your mistakes. Demonstrate that it's what confident people do.
#2: Ditch common sense	Don't expect anyone to know anything. We assume people know what we know. Make it clear we're all at different starting points, and that's okay.
#3: No shaming	Don't make people feel embarrassed for not knowing something. It can prevent them from learning more about a topic.
#4: Remember: it's not personal	We're all wrong from time to time. Remember, it's not a personal flaw; it's a sign of your learning.
	Normalize saying you're sorry when you've hurt someone.

Image 3.1

Idea #12: Do an ego check.

Sometimes we are upset about an issue. Other times, we're so interested in being right or in validating an idea that we lose our *why*. Before engaging with another person, it's worthwhile to take a breath and ask ourselves if we want to be right or if we want to win. Usually, we want to be right. It's about ourselves, and we are looking for a fight to make ourselves feel better. If you want to win, there's usually a bigger goal you want to achieve or a problem you want to solve.

Teaching our students to reflect on the purpose of their arguments can ensure we're doing things for an actual reason beyond ourselves. Here are five steps we can review and follow:

1. Take a deep breath and pause.

2. Reflect: Why does this bother you? What are your goals for engaging with this person about this topic? Is it worth it?

3. Challenge the other person to reflect: Why do they care about this? What argument are they trying to make?

4. Decide if it's worth pursuing: If you realize it's more for your ego, then maybe it's time to take a step back and rethink your goals. If you realize the other person is doing it more for their ego, it also might be a sign to take a step back, as they are not there to learn.

5. Be civil: When you engage in a conversation, be kind. Be respectful to one another as you exchange ideas, or be polite as you bow out.

Idea #13: Help students be happy with themselves.

Sometimes people engage in unproductive, ego-boosting activities because they feel insecure or have low self-esteem. Perhaps helping students understand their self-worth and strengths will enable them to have the confidence to admit when they are not knowledgeable about a topic. Find an outlet to generate awareness (some examples are class discussions, journal prompts, and special self-care days) of the importance of understanding and maintaining a sense of self-worth.

Understand the value of self-care in feeling good.

- Get enough sleep.

- Eat well.

- Exercise.

Be intentional with maintaining a positive self-image.

- Create small goals and complete them.
- Don't compare yourself to others (staying off social media is helpful).
- Spend time with people who energize you and push you to do and be better.

Understand what you bring to the table.

- Reflect on your strengths.
- Tell your story.
- See your growth.

Idea #14: Use debate to help students find their voices.

Helping students find and use their voices is a great way to instill confidence. Debate offers an ideal setting to help students practice using their voices while also providing them with an opportunity to practice discussing issues effectively. Every subject area offers an opportunity for us to engage students in debate and to show we respect their voices and take them seriously.

How this can work:

Option 1: Run a debate that captures the broad view of your class. For example, you could have students form teams around the question: "Why should students learn algebra?" (or any other subject). Divide students into debate teams, with one side defending the affirmative and the other side defending the opposition.

Option 2: Pick a debate that aligns with your class content. This debate could relate to a current event, book, or article assignment.

First, encourage each team to structure their debate as follows:

- Introduction
- Argument:
  - ▶ The claim: State your position.
  - ▶ The data: Cite proof or evidence that backs your claim.
  - ▶ The warrant: Interpret how the data support the claim.
  - ▶ You can have students repeat the claim-data-warrant cycle as you see fit. We recommend two claims.
- Prepare for rebuttals.
- Summarize with a conclusion.

Most debates run on a cycle with two rounds for each team to make an affirmative claim and two rounds for each team to make their rebuttals.

Model civility. Set ground rules for the debate so students understand what it looks like to politely exchange ideas. For instance:

- No ad hominem (personal) attacks.
- Listen carefully to the arguments of your opponent.
- Do not interrupt. Let the other team finish their arguments before you begin.
- Manage your emotions. Don't let your feelings get the best of you.

Idea #15: Use the *Learning for Growth* chart.

Gamify students' personal growth by giving them credit for the times they've uncovered something new. We need to normalize not knowing or being wrong so students internalize that we are all learners. Working with students, list ideas to create a personal success chart where students can monitor and see their growth. Add a reward for a job well done. See Image 3.2 for tally chart ideas.

IDEAS FOR A TALLY CHART

Made a goal and completed it	
Revised an assignment	
Double-checks their knowledge (for example, add a tally for every time a student says, "Let me look that up" or "Let me see where I learned that from.")	
Admits a mistake or if they were wrong	
Says they're sorry if they hurt someone	

Image 3.2

CHAPTER 4

CONSUME INFORMATION MINDFULLY

Create savvy consumers of information with all forms of media and communication

The truth is still the truth, even if no one believes it.
A lie is still a lie, even if everyone believes it.

– UNKNOWN

Essential Question: How do you help students become more critical consumers of information?

Objective: Help students become more informed consumers of information by helping them discern the credibility and expertise of sources.

THE PROBLEM: STUDENTS STRUGGLE TO DISCERN CREDIBLE INFORMATION FROM BOGUS INFORMATION

IMAGINE THAT YOUR friend or loved one sends you another bogus video, this one claiming the Earth is flat. Although your first urge may be to roll your eyes, you know that if you want to fully understand why you received this, you need to take it seriously. Doing your best to model humility, ask them to tell you why they believe so strongly in this idea and why they sent you the video. The sender replies by sending you random articles they found on the internet that are, again, completely bogus. You wonder how they cannot see that, obviously, the leader of the local flat Earth club might not be the most credible source. Now that the person will have a conversation, you wonder how to proceed. It's obvious from the sources you received that this person has difficulties consuming information. It occurs to you that this person just doesn't know how to determine whether a source is credible or if someone is an expert.

You point out to your friend—nicely, of course—that the author of this piece might not be the most credible as they have a background in communications, not science, and that perhaps since virtually 100 percent of the scientific community agrees the world is round, maybe what this person is saying isn't valid. Your friend then responds that the scientific community is in cahoots with the government to instill fear among the masses so we're forced to rely on "the man." You pause the conversation, not knowing how to proceed. Suddenly, this conversation has become completely irrational. You respond by saying that it seems unlikely, to which you then receive back the chiding remark that everyone is entitled to their own opinion.

Once again, your head is spinning. You've graded countless debates and argumentative essays and wonder how this person accepts their performance. Yes, people are entitled to their opinions, but good arguments (whether written or oral) tend to have the same structure. Usually, there's a thesis statement followed by valid supporting arguments that are evidence-based, as well as a logical refute for the opposing party. This person seemed to feel completely justified in formulating an opinion—and backing it—with no sound evidence. Had they still been in school, you could only imagine the grade they would have received for their argument.

You wonder why this might be happening. Why is it that seemingly normal, functioning, nice adults are so unwilling to be swayed, even if their opinions or sources can easily be shown to be invalid? Of course, this is connected to our last chapter focusing on humility, but here in Chapter 4, we examine people's ability to decipher through the accredited versus the bogus in the free-for-all that has become global media.

THE SOLUTION: CONSUME INFORMATION MINDFULLY

Polarization takes on new levels when we can no longer decipher fact from fiction or truth from opinion. When we cannot discern who is an expert (when people hold everyone's opinion on a subject to the same esteem regardless of background or experience), we have a problem. When we can no longer recognize which news outlets still invest in quality journalism, we spiral into a world of uncertainty. Social media compounds the situation because people—who may not have great skills in consuming media information—suddenly become bombarded with new sources. The result is that people cling to whatever resonates with their belief system. And sometimes, the less you know, the more you go out of your way to validate false beliefs. (Another potential impact of the Dunning-Kruger effect previously mentioned.) All of this compounding can lead to the chipping away of our foundations and our very sense of reality.

We've entered a post-truth age where misinformation is widely available (and accepted), and we make political arguments more on emotional appeal than on logic or reason. This alarming phenomenon seems to correspond directly to today's modern media consumption. It's easy to think your worldview is the only (or best) one out there or to find outlets that justify your beliefs (even if it's just a meme). As social media platforms have grown, they have become one of the biggest sources people use to get information. Without adequate skills to discern what's credible and what's not, the line between fact and fiction becomes blurry.

Our goal is to ensure our students are prepared for a world in which misinformation runs rampant. We want them to be prepared to investigate ideas and feel confident that they know who to believe. Understanding how to consume information and discern quality sources is critical to building trust in our institutions. In doing so, we overcome a big obstacle in today's world: posttruth. Mindful information consumption is critical for students to identify credible versus false information so we can, once again, set the bar on truth. Without truth, it is impossible to find a consensus. How can we engage others in problems when they don't believe the problems exist?

CIVICS CONNECTION: MINDFUL INFORMATION CONSUMPTION SUPPORTS A UNIFIED NATION

It's our job to engage students in discussions and political matters in an unbiased way as much as possible. But when we cannot talk about truths—such as climate change or pandemic issues—we've hit a serious wall. In some schools, we've decided it's better to censor (choosing not to discuss or expose students to anything at all) or to make sure we're discussing both sides. The first approach prevents us from teaching vital skills like critical thinking and communication—skills you learn from exposure to new ideas and information.

The second approach forces us to contribute to this post-truth world where anything goes. Unfortunately, there are not always two sides to every story, so justifying falsehoods so we value everyone's opinion is nothing short of unethical. Students can always discuss any issue and entertain any idea, but if they've investigated the issue and concluded that everyone can believe whatever they want despite the overwhelming evidence against an idea, that's a failure of the education system and a direct path toward polarization.

As an example, in the US, during late spring and early summer of 2020, it became unavoidable not to be exposed to a provocative and seemingly authentic video titled *Plandemic*. The video tells the story of a scientist who was being a patriotic whistleblower, supposedly doing her duty to inform the American public that scientists working in the deep state had been benefiting from the onset of the COVID-19 pandemic. The result was that viewers received ammunition to doubt the pandemic, not to take guidelines seriously, and not to trust the government. Many people saw it and simply believed the video's narrative, panicked, and shared it with friends.

Ten million people viewed the video before social media platforms started taking it down because of its false nature, which added fuel to the fire as believers saw this action as the government covering up its tracks. Even though it was apparently a hoax created by a discredited and disgruntled scientist, the damage had been done. Hysteria had emerged. After the dust settled a bit and many people recognized that the video was a hoax, many others still maintained the video was true. For these people, the bogus narrative provided an explanation that gave them comfort, even if it wasn't true.

> *Teaching students to consume information in an age where fact and fiction have become disturbingly blurry to the general population makes our work even harder (and even more important).*

The pandemic was a relevant issue to discuss with our civics students, and the topic led to multiple fruitful discussions. How have countries handled pandemics historically? What strategies are in place? How do we balance our health, our well-being, and the economy? What are other countries doing? What are the responsibilities of citizens? The list goes on. But all in all, this was a chance to discuss how we come together as a nation to tackle a problem.

However, when you must first convince students that the pandemic is *real*, you realize just how many people distrust the government, international organizations, experts, and academics.

To the detriment of society, polarization prevents us from having informed discussions so we can work together to create solutions. Validating false beliefs forces us to waste time on inaction, putting lives at stake.

We can work together to re-establish some standards. Post-truthism lends itself to instability and insecurity because people are unsure who to trust. We must work together to develop that trust in institutions, in knowledge, and in each other. It is critical to keep a nation together, because at what point does the inability of a society to make that important distinction lead to the ultimate fall of that society? That is a terrifying concept to ponder, yet it speaks to the importance of the job we have as teachers. Of course, one of the best ways to do that is to help students learn how to consume information by providing them with the building blocks to clearly discern what's credible and what's not.

MAKE THIS SKILL A REALITY

Now, we're battling the effects of post-truthism firsthand. Every argumentative essay, research report, and debate suddenly provides an opportunity for students to practice source-finding and consuming information. However, in a post-truth world, you face new extremes. Students argue that valid news sources are fake or that certain experts are frauds. We're in a disturbing conundrum where some students—and parents—don't trust us as educators to help students discern credible sources because they believe they have already done their research. Teaching students to consume information in an age where fact and fiction have become disturbingly blurry to the general population makes our work even harder (and even more important).

So how do we teach kids what's fact and what's fabricated? We need to strive to create activities and assessments that encourage students to evaluate sources. At the most basic level, we might encourage students to use metacognitive practices to reflect on where they learned about certain pieces of information. How do they know what they know? Is it valid? On a deeper level, we might rethink our assessments so they facilitate a process where students need to cite sources to validate their ideas and arguments. The more commonplace it becomes to question how we came to our conclusions and what to look for in finding trustworthy sources, the more we internalize strategies to stay competent in our ability to evaluate the constant flow of information that bombards our lives.

These strategies are a nice transition from Chapter 3, which focused on humility. Once students learn how not to wrap their egos around being correct, they're more likely to keep an open mind to new ideas and new resources. They're ready to take part in a learning journey. That journey includes equipping them with strategies to identify which sources and information are most likely to lead to a sound conclusion. As students learn to navigate through what they digest and determine which content is worthwhile or truthful, it is critical we allow them to develop this skill independently, which is most effectively accomplished if done through inquiry.

STRATEGIES YOU CAN IMPLEMENT RIGHT AWAY

Idea #16: Keep reading alive.

Sometimes we hear complaints about the number of people who only watch the news or consume information via social media. It is no secret that newspapers have struggled in recent years, especially local papers. A free press is an important part of democracy.

Print journalism often offers a deeper and wider range of coverage than television. Social media, though vast, offers too much misinformation. It is worthwhile to support young people as savvy readers so they don't fall prey to forms of media that might be easy to digest but are inaccurate or biased.

We've noticed that many students can technically read but have a low comprehension of what they are reading. This may signal a flaw in how we approach reading education. While we know part of this might be a matter of policy, we believe we can take steps to keep a love of reading alive. As we know, the more you read, the more you hone your skills. Here are a few tips to help students associate reading and books with positive time spent:

- *Don't make reading a chore.* Kids naturally love stories, so let them learn at their own pace and read for pleasure. We can kill their love of reading when we constantly force them to over-analyze what they've been reading or constantly ask them to identify the parts of a story.

- *Abandon the competition.* We don't need to pressure our youth to learn to read at an early age. If they like books, that's what counts, and we should praise them for engaging. In Finland, students learn to read in schools at age seven. In Switzerland, they start at age six. In the US, we often encourage young people to start reading much earlier—as young as three or four—with little evidence it helps society members in the long run. It may even deter young readers from wanting to engage with books, as the focus is not on a love of reading but on the societal pressure to read at a certain level based on their age. Let our youngest readers associate books as something positive, not as something they need to prove themselves.

- *Promote a wide range of books.* Let students choose what they want to read. Make books visible in the classroom. Share a wide variety of books with different topics and stories so students can see what they gravitate toward.

- *Let their love for reading naturally evolve.* If students enjoy books and associate reading as a joyful experience, they will continue to practice reading. This improves their skills.

- *Model.* Let your students see you read. Let them see a novel or newspaper on your desk. Let them see you physically holding a book and enjoying reading.

Idea #17: Discern fact versus opinion.

Many struggle to discern fact from opinion, and this goes well into adulthood. Here is a valuable exercise to help students understand the difference between fact and opinion and to consume information more objectively. We've given some basic prompts but suggest you add your own.

Step 1: Review these definitions of fact and opinion:

Fact: Something known to have happened or to exist, especially something about which there is information or for which proof exists.

Opinion: A belief or thought about someone or something.

Step 2: Ask your students to respond to prompts. Here are a few examples:

Human activity has accelerated climate change. This is a fact the scientific community has validated through extensive research.

Lying is always bad. This is an opinion. Some may argue that lying can be positive in certain situations, such as harmless lies.

Manu was the first human on Earth. This is an opinion. While many Hindus believe this, we have no evidence to confirm this is true.

Adam and Eve were the first humans on Earth. This is an opinion. While many Christians believe this, we have no evidence to confirm this is true.

Idea #18: Give an assessment that encourages writing.

Writing sparks critical thinking. It forces you to learn how to evaluate sources, express yourself, and organize your thoughts. Writing encourages students to synthesize information, state positions, and craft rational arguments to support those positions. Often, writing demands that we identify sources to support our work. In examining sources, students must discern the experts from the novices and the credible information from the hoaxes. This idea encourages you, the teacher, to craft at least one assessment or assignment where your students must use sources to validate their work.

Writing challenges force students to investigate the information they consume. Here are three ideas of ways to use writing to help students consume information mindfully.

Current event analysis. Have students submit a summary, reaction, and analysis of the article being explored.

Abandon the multiple choice. Ask students to write an analysis or synthesis of something they've learned, citing resources from class.

Debate claim. Give students a claim and have them craft an argumentative essay to affirm or oppose the claim.

Idea #19: Keep an information consumption tally.

Here's an activity to help students understand the sources they use to gain information. During a group discussion around a current event or issue, have students write three things they believe about the issue. Then ask students, "Where did you learn that from?" using the following list:

- TV
- Social media
- Documentary
- Book
- Newspaper or magazine
- Person (word of mouth, including family, friends, or others)
- Other

Create a chart on the board and ask students to come up and place a tally next to the sources they noted on their paper. This will generate an observable and measurable chart to ponder the significance of where they digest most of their information and what that means for them. Facilitate a group discussion around what you uncover.

Idea #20: Play the *Who's the Expert* activity.

Part 1: Encourage students to reflect on the question: "How do you *know* who to listen to on different topics?"

- Group your students and ask them to create a chart that separates two groups of people: the credible and the non-credible.
- Ask them to list in the columns the cues they look for to know if someone is credible or not, based on several topics.

- These topics are endless but could be things like "Who is a good person to ask questions about home safety tips?" or "Who would be knowledgeable about what is good to feed your pet?" (Of course, make them applicable to your grade and content area.)

- The cues in this activity could be things like someone's occupation, life experiences, and educational opportunities that connect them to a particular topic.

- After the students have reflected on who they feel might be credible or not in the various subjects, you can move the conversation toward media sources.

Part 2: Now encourage students to reflect on this question: "Are the media sources you use credible or not in reporting information?"

- Ad Fontes Media has an interactive media bias chart that explores bias and truth in the media. Assign your students to study this chart in groups.

- Next, after your students have explored this chart, encourage them to develop questions about what the diagram suggests. The key will be to use this chart and your students' questions to hold an open discussion.

- Hopefully, an honest conversation will emerge on topics like fake news, media bias, and agenda setting and what all this means to us as information consumers. Knowing a source's reliability will certainly strengthen your students' awareness of news that may be agenda-oriented and tribal in nature.

CHAPTER 5

AVOID CENSORSHIP

Produce critical thinkers through a variety of outlets, voices, and materials

Censorship is the child of fear and the father of ignorance.
— LAURIE HALSE ANDERSON

Essential Question: How do we embrace and facilitate tough conversations so students learn how to openly communicate about difficult topics?

Objective: Help students strengthen their critical thinking and communication skills so they can have constructive dialogue on any issue.

THE PROBLEM: WE SHIELD OUR YOUTH FROM REALITY, CAUSING A LACK OF PERSPECTIVE AND CRITICAL THINKING

IT WAS JANUARY 2009, and as a department, the eighth-grade social studies team had decided to take advantage of an opportunity to bring our classes together so students could view the State of the Union address, an annual message delivered by the president to the American people each year. This would be President Obama's first State of the Union, and for us social studies teachers, an ideal opportunity to make our classes feel more relevant. Unfortunately, we ended up not being able to show the speech to all our students. To our dismay, parents started calling in. They were concerned that showing President Obama's speech might lend itself to the indoctrination of a liberal ideology, something they feared for their child. (We have little doubt teachers would have faced similar backlash for wanting to show President Trump's address.)

We were all shocked. How could showing a president's speech be an indoctrination of any kind? How did parents think we were supposed to teach the vital skills of critical thinking and communication while censoring reality? The point of social studies is to develop the skills needed to navigate through policy decision options and the choices provided to us in the political world via these skills. Social studies was never intended to be about memorizing basic facts—at least one would hope that is not the case. Why learn about understanding the impact of events, making observations on important shifts and patterns within society, and assessing data if we cannot discuss what's right in front of our faces?

> *We need to expose our children to tough issues and current events so they can understand what is happening in the world.*

In another example, on January 6, 2021, violent riots occurred as a fervent mob raided Capitol Hill in Washington, DC. It's an understatement to say that this event disturbed the nation. As a response, our school staff sent an email showing we needed to proceed with great caution regarding how to discuss the events of that day. The message was that the storming of the US Capitol was complex and delicate. It was an interesting and bizarre email that many of us interpreted as some sort of attempt to suffocate our voice on how to address it, as though it may be best not to discuss it at all, even in a classroom environment, so as not to offend anyone. Students knew what was going on. They wanted—*needed*—a space to discuss what was happening. Why was the classroom, especially a civics classroom, not the space to have these sorts of conversations?

THE SOLUTION: AVOID CENSORSHIP

Polarization increases when we allow others to censor information and discourage conversations rather than deal with issues head-on. Unfortunately, concealing or pretending tough topics do not exist does little to help our youth solve the problems they will inherit. Just because we choose not to discuss something, to act as if it's not happening, doesn't make the issue go away. We need to expose our children to tough issues and current events so they can understand what is happening in the world.

From there, they can learn to express themselves, articulate ideas, and communicate with one another. Without that exposure and dialogue, the issue can fester. Unspoken words lead to tension and can create pent-up frustration that might unexpectedly appear years later. What's worse, when we don't learn how to communicate, it might instigate people to lash out in unconstructive ways. Avoiding tough conversations compounds problems, as our lack of dialogue causes the initial problem to grow stronger. Without the practice of navigating tough conversations, we grow up unequipped with the skills needed to effectively communicate a path forward.

If we don't allow open, honest, and even tough and unfiltered talk in a safe (or brave) space such as an academic classroom, then we should not act surprised when polarization occurs. Avoiding topics where people feel an injustice or are closed off from new ideas or perspectives only causes further rifts in society. Without communication, we stop learning and understanding. This can lead to the prevalence of misconceptions and assumptions that merit further exploration for students to fully understand. If we don't provide these opportunities to expand their knowledge, we should not act surprised when there is division. When we suppress the opportunity for students to explore their world, we should not act surprised when they find solace in those who think like them and not in those who challenge them to learn more.

Students need a chance to "practice like they'll play" so they turn into adults who can effectively communicate and discuss complicated issues. Without this practice, students might face many repercussions. Some might lose their voices and turn into adults who become too afraid of what others might think. Others might succumb to emotional tribalism, where they get caught in what they believe in and root for those beliefs at all costs, as opposed to seeking the truth and doing what is right, whether or not it supports one's belief system. Others might not learn strategies to engage with those who don't think like them and resort to attacking or shaming, thus breaking down any form of communication.

But the reality of it is that the stifling of communication that leads to polarization isn't at all a natural characteristic within us. (Think back to Chapter 2, which deals with our curiosity.) Most students want to talk about issues, at least at the onset of their school experience. If we're nurturing students' curiosity, we'll realize that, naturally, their questions will become more complicated, more ambiguous, and more philosophical as they work to understand the intricacies of the world. Are we embracing these opportunities? If not, what are we scared of?

We can't afford to shut down the questions that come organically from being a living person who notices what's happening in the world around them. It's part of the sense-making each student experiences as they deepen their understanding of the world. We then deny them the opportunity to speak about topics we're supposed to avoid. We might also kill their curiosity and confidence. (Remember the University of Michigan study that found evidence that students ask fewer questions as they get older?) If you're not allowed to ask questions, it's no wonder that, over time, you stop asking.

Of course, teachers are concerned about this potential killing of curiosity, as we know many of the censored conversations are the very ones that students need and want to have. Every teacher can vouch that a student has come in with a heavy question; it's just that we're often unsure how to address it. The world around students affects them, and many need a space to talk about how they feel or to get a better understanding of why that issue or event is happening. School might be their only outlet to learn about issues and engage with new feelings and ideas. Other than their primary guardians, students consider their teachers as some of the most important adult role models in their lives. Teachers might be a last line of defense for their students to gain the skills and knowledge to discern controversial issues, which brings us to another reality we deal with as teachers: parental pushback.

We understand you might receive backlash from parents, your administration, or your community, but you can't afford to censor every issue that might cause controversy. They're often too important to avoid. We can't assume students have a deep understanding of issues or that they'll have a chance to learn about them elsewhere. There is no such thing as common sense (we'll discuss this in more detail later) or a level playing field for our students. They might not realize a comment they make sounds ignorant or prejudiced. They might be ignorant, and that's okay because that's what they came to school for: to learn. We encourage and challenge you to keep doing what it takes to nourish our students, even if this pushback is powerful and maybe even threatening.

Questions, critical thought, creativity, reflection, self-examination, and communication—none of these can happen when we censor. If you know something is in the best interest of the students, please don't feel guilty or fearful about facilitating that conversation. For those who question you, challenge them. How can we expect our students to learn to be critical thinkers who can work together if we avoid the issues and never give students the opportunity to embrace the real world? We can't. Teachers shouldn't have to defend themselves for doing their job to ensure students receive a quality education.

CIVICS CONNECTION: DON'T BE AFRAID TO DISCUSS TOUGH TOPICS

As we stated earlier, students need to practice like they'll play. There's nothing worse than watching adults on television yelling at and insulting each other over an issue. That's not what good communication looks like, and that's not how we solve problems. We need to have civil conversations on tough topics, a skill we should practice in the classroom so we can apply it as adults. We need to set up our classrooms to ensure these conversations can and will occur. We can't emphasize it enough: if we avoid talking about politics (and even religion) in school, then we will end up with a society that can't talk about politics and religion. We have that now, and it's causing stagnation.

Censoring every issue that is deemed controversial has forced many teachers to attempt teaching with their hands tied. We ask that learning be relevant and that students gain skills for the real world, but too often, if we allow students to engage in issues, we feel a weight on our shoulders like we've done the wrong thing. Hearing from upset parents should not deter us from doing our jobs, although we know it's stressful to have to consistently explain yourself. We must practice communication, especially how to have a constructive and civil dialogue on the topics that matter.

In the civics classroom, we discuss all the tough stuff, including religion, racism, equity, economics, sustainability, and law. If done properly, our curriculum covers everything most people want to avoid. But that's the beauty of not only civics but social studies. It's the study of the world, its people, and how it's all interconnected. What could be more relevant than that?

Unfortunately, though, social studies classes are often electives. We may only offer a civics class for four months of a student's entire academic career. Where, then, can students discuss what's happening in the world and explore issues dear to them? We should not think of worldly affairs as only relevant for the four months we spend on them in our classes. The world doesn't stop, which is why we need to provide outlets that ensure students learn to communicate effectively about tough topics. Within any class, regardless of the subject or grade level, we bring in more relevancy and enable students to find their voices and explore the issues of today.

We believe the mantra for any classroom should be to let students practice like they'll play. We can't assume they know certain things—what we think of as common sense. When something is relevant, we must give them space to discuss it so we normalize communication and thoughtful conversations with people, even when we disagree with them—especially when we disagree with them. As educators, isn't that what we all want? We must be brave enough to try.

MAKE THIS SKILL A REALITY

When we discuss relevant subjects in the classroom, students want to know why things are happening out there. *Why is the world unfair? Why are people so hateful?* Tough conversations give our students the opportunity to embrace difficult topics and to communicate and articulate thoughts. Allowing them to discuss complex issues and exposing them to a wide range of materials and perspectives helps them tap into their morals and ethics and those of others. It helps them understand their purpose and create a vision for how they think the world should be.

Avoiding censorship signals the opening up of dialogue. Communication should be one of the easier skills to facilitate in the classroom as long as students know they have a space where it is okay to talk about anything. Exchanging ideas should be a core part of learning, regardless of content area or grade level. World events constantly offer a narrative to bring meaning and relevance to any subject area. It's in how we facilitate learning that we might craft opportunities to practice communication skills. Communication is not just oral but also includes how we assess, how we use technology, and what or how we write. Learning happens not from engaging in controversial or censored materials but from giving students opportunities to articulate and exchange their ideas around the topic.

It's critical we use as many outlets as possible. Too often, we think of communication as having a full-class discussion. It doesn't always need to look this way, and often this format for discussion leaves out most students' voices. For instance, crafting a relevant problem-based learning project might force students to engage in complicated dialogue with one another around an issue. Asking students to write an email about what they feel or use social media to engage in a discussion can help them practice how to apply their tech skills to "do good." Pairs, fishbowls, writing exercises, and art—teaching opportunities abound for us to create moments where they might practice communicating. The main barrier is to offer that space for students to engage with one another.

Day-to-day interactions and random questions posed by students might also offer us windows to embrace needed dialogues. We may get so focused on the curriculum that we forget that children have questions about life. They are growing up and learning, and everyday life is a part of their experience. The more relevant school is, the more they will see the applications in the world around them. It's only natural they want to talk about what's happening to them.

STRATEGIES YOU CAN IMPLEMENT RIGHT AWAY

Idea #21: Advocate for the end of over-censoring.

More and more, we're not allowed to discuss current events or religion or recognize certain holidays, which leaves important topics unexplored and doesn't encourage or promote tolerance. So let's be advocates for opening up topics, not closing them down.

Too often, there is a fear of the unknown. For example, social media isn't going anywhere. Instead of helping students apply their skills and learn how to use technology for the common good (such as through platforms like YouTube or TikTok), there is often a tendency to ban it. Other times, we fear a conversation will get misconstrued or that a film or book might offend, so we justify the ban.

We wonder, though, if we've gone too far in the quest to shield our children from reality. Is banning Mark Twain's *The Adventures of Huckleberry Finn* because it uses the N-word the best way to teach our students about race relations? Or is exploring the book and the clear message of advocating racial tolerance a better method? Why are we banning *The Hate U Give* by Angie Thomas? Is it promoting an anti-police message or just highlighting obvious flaws in our society? These questions are rhetorical. It's okay to not have the answers. Are these not great issues to discuss with your students?

We created this teacher's checklist to determine whether censoring an item is taking it too far:

- Is it factual?

- Does it promote critical thinking?

- Does it help show multiple perspectives, or can you use it to discuss multiple perspectives, arguments, and critiques?

- Does it embrace reality (past, present, or future)?

The more check marks, the more we shouldn't feel guilty about engaging our students in the material that can make them question and explore their world.

Idea #22: Create a brave space.

The safe space makes us feel all warm and cozy, but uncomfortable topics that push our thinking make us uncomfortable. We simply cannot continually avoid being uncomfortable. Having discomfort can be positive for student growth if it's harnessed in the right arena. We need to press on and have those conversations because they make us better people. A great way to do this is to advocate for the brave space, not the safe space.

Get this started with students by setting parameters for your brave space. What will it look like? What are their expectations? What ground rules would they set? See if you can craft an agreement together.

Idea #23: Ditch the plans.

We need to get better at letting organic conversations take their course and nurturing them. Kids want to know about well-being, mental health, and what's right and wrong, and we need to accept that this type of learning is often more valuable than what's in the curriculum. It's okay to be fluid and adaptable when the moments occur. You're giving your students what they need when they need it.

That said, we understand that teachers have a curriculum to get through, and valuable conversations might ignite at inconvenient moments. For that reason, try to provide multiple outlets for students to communicate. If you're comfortable with these, here are some outlets you might explore:

Email. Let students know they can contact you via email with questions, and you can address them that way.

School messenger app. Many schools have a social media platform where students might direct their questions. If yours does, let them know they can reach you through that outlet.

Calendly. Set office hours and use a scheduling app like Calendly so students can arrange to meet with you one-on-one, both during school hours and via video conferencing software, such as Zoom.

For some, it might be too embarrassing to speak up in front of the class, so let's provide as many outlets as possible for students to ask those taboo questions they want to discuss. These outlets also help those students too intimidated to speak out and those who need more time to reflect.

Idea #24: Help students navigate sensationalism.

Sensationalized stories often spark our interest because they target our emotions. How can we identify if we are falling prey to sensationalism? Being able to think objectively about an issue or situation helps us to lower the temperature and think more critically.

Here are a few current top issues in the US that can immediately cause people to get up in arms:

- Is immigration the key issue right now?
- Are gender-nonspecific bathrooms acceptable?
- Will the government take away our guns?

These issues can cause an emotional response to flare and often lead to binary thinking. Instead, we can help students be aware of and fight sensationalism by helping them explore facts around an issue. Encourage students to investigate headlines from recognized news sources. This could be a story or even surveys or other forms of tabled data. Task students with determining whether the story is accurate or not by collaborating to further investigate and assess the issue. Questions posed might include:

- Are there any signs that we have sensationalized this issue? How do you know?

- Is there suggestive language as to how you should feel about the issue? Describe it.

- How many people does the issue impact?

- Is the content realistic? What would it look like to take action on the content? Is it possible? (For example, we're not going to de-fund the police.)

Debrief with students. Did they consider the piece sensationalized? How did they come up with their conclusions?

Idea #25: Inspire student journalism.

The goal of investigative journalism is not to go in with the answers but to see where the truth leads you. When students come up with an emotional topic, encourage them to act as journalists so they might investigate the accuracy and urgency of the issue. Let them research. Let them talk to people. Let them observe. Let them listen. Have them package their findings in an article or video (for example, their own news broadcast).

CHAPTER 6

EMBRACE COMPLEXITY
Stop oversimplifying difficult issues

*Don't define your world in black and white because
there is so much hiding among the greys.*
— FATIMAH SHALASH

Essential Question: How do we get students to dive deeper into topics so they see the world through multiple lenses?

Objective: Help students learn the harm of oversimplification. Embracing complexity helps us uncover how not to make assumptions that lead to misconceptions.

THE PROBLEM: PERPETUATING MISINFORMATION, LABELS, ASSUMPTIONS, AND STEREOTYPES THROUGH OVERSIMPLIFICATION

IT WAS MY (Michelle's) first Girl Scout meeting as the leader of my daughter's troop. The cafeteria was full of other troop leaders discussing upcoming events and opportunities that we might take part in. Someone mentioned World Thinking Day, a one-day event when Girl Scouts from all over the world are to think of one another and celebrate each other. Curious about what this entailed, the person who ran last year's event summarized the activities they had done the prior year. Apparently, the focus had been on Switzerland, with participating troops eating Swiss food and dressing in traditional Swiss costumes.

This made me wonder how dressing up in traditional attire was helping the girls to understand Swiss culture as it is today. Being married to someone from Switzerland and having lived in the country multiple times, I was a bit amused by the mismatch between the activities of the day and the realities of what the present-day culture is like. Many people have asked me if I speak Swiss (there's no such thing), so I could not help but question how we help our young people to gain perspective by showing such an inaccurate portrayal. Did other countries have students dress up as Pilgrims when learning about the United States? How was focusing on archaic traditions, teaching children that countries still operated as they did a hundred years ago, acceptable as cultural understanding? This was a lack of understanding coupled with an oversimplification of the culture.

That said, we love the Girl Scouts, and this in no way should reflect poorly on them. We've seen this repeatedly in the education space both inside and outside the classroom (and have surely been guilty of this ourselves): an oversimplification of complex issues and topics. We go in with the best of intentions but somehow end up perpetuating the stereotypes we grew up with. It may be because we think we know more about something than we actually do or because we want to make the subject easier to understand. Oversimplification strips away the depth and accuracy we want to encourage our students to embrace.

We live in a world of misconceptions, assumptions, and labeling. It's our attempt to categorize and simplify that which is incredibly complex. However, this leads us to another key ingredient of polarization: tribalism. Modern tribalism is a sociological concept in which people organize themselves into social groups with those who share their attitudes and behaviors. When we go through life perpetuating stereotypes and putting people, places, and issues into these arbitrary boxes, the world suddenly looks very black and white.

The more we simplify, the more we create these labels, and the more we find ourselves in a polarized world. Most everything falls somewhere in the gray zone between black and white. Simplification often forces us to focus on the superficial when people, places, and issues are complex and deep. In doing so, we lose sight of the fact that we have more in common with others than we believe.

THE SOLUTION: EMBRACE COMPLEXITY

To embrace complexity, we must get comfortable with not having all the answers and acknowledge there are no absolutes. Switzerland has four national languages and many cultural differences throughout its regions. As with any culture, there are variances and outliers, plus cultures are always in a state of change. Who yodels anymore?

Fortunately, when we embrace complexity, it can help us find the thread that unites us. When looking at a culture that is new to us, it's helpful to remember we are all people. Most humans want health and happiness. They strive to put food on the table and have a decent quality of life. They want to feel safe and ensure their children have a good future. Instead of putting labels on a culture, it can be more useful to explore how other societies work to achieve those goals. What can we learn from how people from other countries act and how their societies tackle similar challenges?

Dealing with complexity can help us become better critical thinkers. It can help us uncover our biases and expose areas in which we need a bit more perspective. When we go beyond the usual oversimplifications or at least know to be skeptical if something comes across as too easy or nicely packaged, it can help us gain a new lens on the world and push our thinking. If we practice humility and remember there's always more to learn and that it's not possible for anyone to have it all figured out, it can help us open our minds.

Here's an example: I (Michelle) became aware in graduate school that Africa was the only continent where people morphed all the countries into one. This had never occurred to me until a professor challenged everyone in my class to name ten countries in Africa. Most people couldn't complete the task, which is difficult to believe as there are fifty-six countries to choose from. We were then told that most people in the West didn't even realize Africa had modern cities. That not only were the countries blurred into one, but most people described Africa as a place of huts and poverty and left it at that.

When I began teaching sociology, I would pose this question to students: What's Africa like? I was almost never called out on it. No one asked me which country I was referring to, much less any specific town or region. Then, to prove my professor's point, my students would speak of lions and huts. I would then show them a picture of Johannesburg in South Africa or Addis Ababa in Ethiopia, and it dumbfounded them. They didn't realize there were modern cities, just like anywhere else. How harmful to lump together fifty-six nations as one, as if the countries and cultures within don't have enough merit to deserve recognition. The implications of this at a macro level should be obvious. It's a continent that often gets overlooked.

Of course, this happens on a micro level as well and can be detrimental to the well-being of those around us. Humans are complex beings. Do we take time to get to know the whole person? Even in schools, we check off boxes labeling our youth by their gender, race, and religion as if that's all that matters. Is this how we want young people to define themselves? Not by their ethics, values, morals, talents, strengths, knowledge, and overall uniqueness, but only by superficial designations? Viewing or labeling our students as "different" can cause so much harm.

This is a great opportunity for us to let our guards down a bit to admit and discuss how our views have not always paid attention to individual differences. Along those lines, I (Brian) often share a story with my students from years ago that I believe lets students realize we are all capable of falling into the detrimental assumptions that stem from simplistic labeling.

It was the summer of 2008, and we took our then-two-year-old children to St. Louis, Missouri, to visit the famous Gateway Arch. As we waited in line, I noticed two men ahead of me who seemed out of place. Both men were fidgety, by my estimation, as though they were up to something. In my mind, I deemed these guys to be threatening because they were young (in their twenties), they were not with families, and they appeared to be of Middle Eastern descent. As I tell the story, I admit to my students that it was the latter characteristic that was most pressing in my thoughts as I stood there with my family. Remember, I lived through the moments of 9/11. I lived through the hysteria and fear, along with the unity and resolve, and unfortunately, the Islamophobia that emerged.

As the line of people moved ahead and the men got into the elevators, I remember thinking to myself that I should turn around and not go up the Arch. I remember thinking these men could be terrorists and they could destroy this landmark and my family. I didn't let this moment of hysteria change our plans. We went up the Arch and experienced the views.

Afterward, I used the drive home to reflect intensely on what was going on in my mind. The intense labeling that Middle Easterners have received since the 9/11 attack unquestionably shaped my thoughts. I vowed to do better in assessing individuals and situations. When I share this story with my classes, I'm making myself vulnerable to encourage them to reflect more on the assumptions and labels they may have embraced that can be damaging and polarizing.

Complexity enables us to view situations through multiple lenses and challenges us to go beyond the superficial and gain a deeper understanding. When we strive to simplify, when we surrender to labels and assumptions, we can perpetuate harmful thoughts and behaviors. What if I had embraced my initial biases driven by my cultural experiences regarding the two Middle Eastern men? I could have become an active bigot toward them in that moment by calling them out or confronting them. That's not what we want for ourselves, and that's not what we want to pass on to our students.

> *Political figures around the world have taken advantage of labeling people and oversimplifying issues for their own advantage. We have to dismantle this in the classroom.*

To prevent polarization, we must strive to gain a deeper understanding of our world. We must equip ourselves and our students with the tools to see our limitations. In this way, we continue to grow and learn together. This may feel uncomfortable. This may require vulnerability, but that's part of where humility and curiosity come into play. Do we fully understand the world as we know it? Will we admit it if we don't? It's disconcerting to learn that the reality we thought we knew isn't as it seems. These examples might make us squirm, but it's okay to feel discomfort. We invite you to lean in and know that it's a normal part of the process.

CIVICS CONNECTION: ALL ISSUES ARE MORE COMPLEX THAN WE THINK THEY ARE

In civics, we're used to dealing with misconceptions, labeling, assumptions, and a massive oversimplification of complex issues.

It's our job to help students dig deeper into issues and provide them with multiple lenses through which to view and explore topics. Bumper sticker politics have made this especially challenging. Social media and the prominence of memes have helped students feel overly confident in their understanding of issues and have contributed to the tribalism mentioned earlier. It's made us wonder how we can help students understand ambiguity and recognize when they've been presented with an oversimplification of an issue, view, or understanding of a topic that's complex.

As soon as we mention a topic like immigration, students automatically put themselves into one of two camps: either for or against. It can be shocking, as few issues dealing with immigration are so trivial. Once we provide some context with a driving question, the conversation suddenly takes on a new light. Should there be a quota on immigration, and if so, what should that be? How do you help immigrants to best integrate into a new system? How do you provide different types of visas, and should they be based on skills (remember, some countries are desperately seeking immigrants with PhDs)? How should a country assist refugees? Suddenly, the conversation shifts from the simplistic "good versus bad" to a real exploration of the issues, what's currently taking place, and ideas on what could be.

Unsurprisingly, we must deal with these oversimplifications on virtually every issue. Misconceptions abound, such as the one that implies we must choose between the environment or business or that if you belong to a certain political party, you have to think a certain way. With every issue, we have to break it up by providing context and a driving question to give purpose to the argument so students can dig deeper and truly explore the intricacies of a complex issue. Our goal is that by the time they leave the classroom, they understand that most issues are much more complex than they seem.

Unfortunately, assumptions, labels, and thinking one-dimensionally cause fear and raise prejudices in our culture that the political world can manipulate. Political figures around the world have taken advantage of labeling people and oversimplifying issues for their own advantage. We have to dismantle this in the classroom. Unsurprisingly, those students with more exposure to diverse perspectives often have an easier time challenging what they don't know and looking more deeply for the truth.

We included this chapter to ensure we all do our part in the classroom and beyond not to perpetuate the misconceptions that cause harm. We should be on a constant quest to provide more perspective. We can ask good driving questions so students understand the purpose and goals behind discussing certain issues. What's the purpose of asking if immigration is good or bad since it's based on opinion, not fact? They should understand that, based on the context of the situation, the dialogue might radically change, and that's okay. There's no one-size-fits-all solution for anything. Let's ensure we're not pushing our own agenda and that we're using words appropriately so we don't skew students' understanding.

This creates an impact. When we misuse words or throw them around carelessly without fully understanding their meaning or scope, polarization can increase. Here's an example: Does socialism equal communism? One of my (Brian's) daughters came home from school recently, upset about a conversation her teacher was having in her eighth-grade social studies class. The teacher asked the class, "Do you like capitalism or socialism better?" Without giving the students an opportunity to explore the question and investigate it on their own, the teacher quickly answered the question himself with clear favoritism toward capitalism and a targeted smear on socialism. He proclaimed socialism as a much worse economic system because it was associated with communism. And communism is bad, even evil.

Growing up in western Europe, my daughter has had a different experience of what socialism means. She lived in Switzerland. She visited all the Scandinavian countries. She learned firsthand what socialism could look like in a democratic, not autocratic, society. Socialistic programs like universal healthcare, pension programs, and public education models mesh into the economic structure of free market capitalism in these countries, which is similar to the way the system is in America.

The difference, and the reason this issue of labeling someone a socialist is so polarizing, has to do with America's inability to make the more complex realization that they operate in a hybrid economic model. One-dimensional labeling of socialism only generates fear, which creates polarization that strengthens tribalism. My daughter's teacher's simplistic labeling of the concept of socialism limited the students' understanding of it on that occasion to their detriment. Will these students ever learn more about this issue in a more complex manner, or will they continue to hold on to this erroneous label as adults?

Undeniably, this is dangerous and has done plenty of harm in many ways already. As teachers, we need to fight this. Let's push our students and ourselves as educators to move beyond one-dimensional thinking.

MAKE THIS SKILL A REALITY

From an early age, we are taught this notion of right versus wrong, of good versus bad. Apart from mathematical calculations and hard science, the world is often not as straightforward as it seems. Unfortunately, simplifying is often the easiest path. It's easier to package a topic or an issue in a lesson or on a social media post in a more surface-oriented manner. This may help us frame the issues in a way people can digest, but does it promote the deeper understandings and intricacies of the issues? As educators, we should challenge ourselves to find opportunities where we can help students navigate ambiguity and go deeper with their learning. Every subject area offers the opportunity for students to embrace complexity. Driving questions, exploring what words mean, and offering various perspectives are all avenues to help students approach problems and issues in new ways.

Having those teaching moments of honesty is certainly one way we can discuss how labeling can polarize our classrooms. Of course, there are other possibilities. The following ideas can help reduce the detriments that can develop from labels and assumptions.

STRATEGIES YOU CAN IMPLEMENT RIGHT AWAY

Idea #26: Recognize stereotypes and labels with the *Meet in the Middle* game.

Too often, it can feel like we have an obsession with labeling everyone and everything. Our idea is for you to constantly remind yourself, "Don't judge a book by its cover." We don't want to make assumptions or force identity by putting kids into arbitrary boxes. Of course, most people don't fit neatly into a box. We want to show students that it's okay to think one way about one issue and another way about another issue. It's best to discuss an issue, not label people and then predetermine how they should think based on that label. Here's a game to help facilitate this conversation. We also offer this on our website: civicsthroughplay.com.

How to Play:

> *Step 1*: Ask students if they identify as an introvert or an extrovert. Ask them to line up on opposing walls based on their selection.
>
> *Step 2*: Tell students that you will ask them five questions. For every question they largely agree with, they

should take a step toward the opposing wall. Be sure to pause between questions so students can reflect.

1. Do you sometimes like to go to parties?

2. Is there an activity you enjoy doing all by yourself?

3. Are you comfortable being in large groups?

4. Do you feel energized after getting some peace and quiet?

5. Do you enjoy socializing with friends at lunch?

Step 3: Ask students to observe where everyone is in the room. What do they notice? Where is everyone standing? Do they still feel like they are one thing or another?

Step 4: Ask students if they've heard of an ambivert. Mention that it's a person who exhibits both introvert and extrovert tendencies. Ask students to think about why they categorized themselves as an extrovert or introvert. Ask a few students to share their answers. Do they still feel that description is accurate?

Step 5: Ask students the following debrief questions:

1. How did it feel to be on opposing walls?

2. What happened when we dug a little deeper? Did we have more in common than we initially thought?

3. Did you find it beneficial to label yourselves as introverts or extroverts? If so, how?

4. Do you see any dangers in us labeling ourselves? If so, what?

5. As a society, do we label ourselves in other ways? What are the consequences of such labeling?

Idea #27: Get accurate with cultural days.

If we are going to celebrate cultural identification days, let's do them right. Instead of the typical exploration of simplistic elements of culture, things like foods, holidays, everyday rituals, and language, let's promote going deeper into the dynamics of a country or culture. Globalization has radically changed the world in which we live, and culture is complex everywhere. We live in a highly interconnected society full of smart people. Propagating archaic aspects of a culture that are no longer practiced can give a false impression to our students. We have so much to learn from one another. For the next cultural day, prompt your students with higher-level questions:

- Look up your country on the HDI (Human Development Index). In which areas do they do well?

- What is this country or culture known for? What do they do well?

- What can we learn from this country or culture?

- How does this country or culture tackle or approach similar problems (for example, pollution, poverty, or food security)?

- What are some taboos from this country or culture?

- What else?

Idea #28: Play the *Digital Pen Pal* activity.

We all know this activity. Growing up, pen pals were often a method our teachers would use to help us get to know other people.

So, let's not get rid of the pen pal effort. It's easier to diminish an "us versus them" mentality when we can place a face behind the unknown. Bringing in the experiences of someone your students are getting to know more deeply is great for showing there's more than one way to do things and live life. Pen pals can broaden our minds and our understanding of others' minds. Fortunately, it's become easier than ever to connect our students to others around the country and around the world. Platforms like PenPal Schools offer an opportunity for students to interact with students from other cultures and countries. Try it out.

Idea #29: Get used to "Googling," and clarify terms objectively and effectively by promoting a *Word of the Week*.

Do we understand the words we're using? Of course, this idea fits with the story mentioned earlier regarding a middle school teacher discussing socialism. Implementing a Word of the Week is a great way to help us and our students navigate nuanced words. Put it on your board or feature it on your school web platform. Provide an outlet for students to investigate or discuss the word through an assignment or as a class discussion.

Word of the Week example for upper grades:

> *Socialism.* This is a continually misunderstood word in American culture. Western Europeans have a much different understanding of this word and its relationship to a free market economy compared to those in the United States. Why is that? They both fought the same Cold War against communist ideals. Why do Europeans view the concepts of socialism in a less threatening and more democratic way than many in the United States?

Freedom. What is freedom, exactly? Is it the ability to do whatever you want regardless of the consequence to others? For instance, is one exercising freedom if they refuse to wear a mask? Does that impact others' freedom to feel safe when out during a pandemic?

Values. What does this mean? How do you define them? Does everyone have the same values?

Word of the Week example for lower grades:

Hero. What makes someone a hero? What is their persona?

Success. What does success mean to you? What do you think it means to your parents? Does everyone have the same definition?

Strength. What does it mean to be strong? How can people have different types of strengths?

Idea #30: Explore political ideology through role-play.

Use a town hall-style role-playing simulation to enable students to explore different types of political ideologies. Students will have to imagine they are candidates running for office.

Step 1: Assign students a political viewpoint: 1) a far-left progressive, 2) a left-center moderate progressive, 3) a centrist, 4) a right-center moderate conservative, and 5) a far-right conservative.

Step 2: Students will have to research three to five topics to help them form an opinion and view based on their assigned roles. Category examples include the economy; national, state, or local security; foreign affairs; global concerns; ethical issues; and specific topics geared toward the different job responsibilities (president, congressperson, governor) and level of government (federal, state, local).

Step 3: Students will develop a platform and philosophy based on the role of their candidate. This will include specific things they want to accomplish as a political figure, why they believe these things to be important, and how they have impacted the candidate to get involved as a political figure.

Step 4: Students will craft a campaign speech and deliver it to the class. They must respect the other views, and they must follow their role even if it's not true to their actual views.

CHAPTER 7

PROMOTE COLLECTIVE LEADERSHIP

Help students uncover their unique roles in contributing to areas greater than themselves

Alone we can do so little; together we can do so much.
— HELEN KELLER

Essential Question: How do we help students understand the importance and impact of their individual actions?

Objective: Create awareness of students' responsibilities toward the greater good. The future is now. Help them to feel accountable for the unique role each will play.

THE PROBLEM: STUDENTS DON'T REALIZE HOW MUCH OUR INDIVIDUAL ACTIONS MATTER AND CONTRIBUTE TO THE WHOLE

THERE IS A story about a teacher who filled the school hallway with balloons. Each balloon had a different student's name written on it. When he asked students to find the balloon with their name, no one could find their balloon. When he asked them to take a balloon and give it to the person whose name was on it, everyone quickly had their balloon. This simple exercise clearly demonstrates the power of teamwork. We are undeniably better off when we look out for others.

In a time when self-absorption and individualism are the norms, we can't help but wonder if we might do better to instead be advocates for unity and collectivism for the greater good. We don't get to pick the era in which we are born or what the world will demand from us. If we've learned anything from recent events like the pandemic, many of the problems we face are wicked problems that impact us all. A wicked problem is complex and has no clear definition, and we can never fully solve it. Most policy problems, such as the United Nations Sustainable Development Goals, fall into this category. Often referred to as the "world's to-do list," these seventeen interrelated goals act as a blueprint to outline the most pressing areas we, as a society, need to address to create a better and more sustainable world.

We mention it because, despite the complexity of these problems, no one person will ever be able to solve them. However, our combined actions will create a tremendous impact. Do our actions do harm, or do they do good?

THE SOLUTION: PROMOTE COLLECTIVE LEADERSHIP

We often think of collective leadership as the process through which individuals come together to create change. It is when people use their unique strengths to build relationships with one another and do their part to contribute toward a shared goal. Of course, it is not a new concept or phenomenon. Throughout history, we have seen examples of the importance and necessity of people working together collectively. How could the Allies in World War II defeat the Axis powers without a collective attitude of mutual involvement and effort among the nations involved?

On the other hand, what has happened recently to diminish the value of collectivism and increase polarization? As we mentioned, some might suggest that the increase in social media has prompted a more individualistic and self-gratifying existence. We're not entirely sure what diminished our sense of togetherness, but we know it doesn't have to be that way. We also know that this shift in mindset from a focus on the self to a focus on the whole lays the foundation for creating good and thoughtful citizens. It is also a critical starting point to develop the last few chapters of this book.

A sports analogy supporting the importance of a collective spirit comes to mind. A basketball player might prefer playing forward, but she serves the team best at guard. We expect the player to accept that position as a member of the sports team. How is this different from living collectively in society? This analogy might make people think more about wearing a mask during a pandemic or adhering to water restrictions when in place. Collectivist contributions encourage us to think about how our actions benefit the whole and ourselves as well. For example, if you're asked to wear a mask to protect others, what's the harm in complying? In being considerate of the health of others, you're doing more to protect yourself as well.

Although it is a nice thought and a virtuous goal to want to live in a harmonious society where we all help each other, that isn't a practical way of looking at how we should advocate for collectivism. It's interesting, but too often, we think doing good or doing something for the community requires a sort of altruism. It doesn't. By working together, we're often not just helping others but achieving better outcomes for our communities at large, and we as individuals also reap the benefits. In the balloon example, not only were all balloons distributed to the right students (thus problem solved), but individuals were also happier because they each received their balloon. There's power in caring for one another. Regardless of the motive, it's in our best interest to invest in collectivism. We achieve more and are often happier individuals, even if it's not always obvious.

Look at litter reduction. In many places around the world, it has become unacceptable to throw your trash on the ground or along the roadside. Although for many of us, it would seem shocking to think about nonchalantly throwing your wrapper out the window of your car or directly on the ground, but it was pretty common practice not so long ago. And why not? It's more convenient to just toss your trash wherever you want. However, for society, the buildup of trash caused other problems. Litter can contribute to pests and diseases. It can harm animals and nature, and let's be honest: it doesn't look nice. When people started understanding the benefits of keeping it clean for all of us, individual behaviors changed, which, when done en masse, led to a much greater impact.

> *Given the problems in the world, we cannot afford to waste time fighting with each other about what matters. Issues that impact us all should unite us all.*

We go further together. Like a vehicle, a society is a collection of individual parts that all rely on one another to function. Have we lost sight of this in recent years? Elements like social media have created more instant gratification and increased selfish behavior. Consider fast fashion, coupled with features like same-day delivery services, and how they have made it easier than ever to shop, but does the rampant consumerism make us feel good about ourselves or help the environment? We are fighting toxic individualism that is not only dividing us but also making us less happy. At a time when we feel pressure to have a platform to emphasize our importance to the world or to mindlessly continue with our habits, we may miss the boat on what truly matters.

We're living in an age where we need to work together to solve the problems that will inevitably impact us all. And there are invisible threats all around us that we might not be aware of but in which our actions play an invaluable role. For example, COVID-19 was not a surprise. We have long hailed pandemics as one of the deadliest threats to humanity, with many calling for preventive measures. We ignored these pleas, and we've all just lived through the consequences. We got lucky this was a mild disease. What happens if the next pandemic is much more deadly?

There are so many issues, and we may feel that our efforts are just a drop in the bucket, but when we collectively take action, the bucket overflows. When society faces a problem and does nothing, we will each feel the impact eventually. Given the problems in the world, we cannot afford to waste time fighting with each other about what matters. Issues that impact us all should unite us all. It's critical that we are aware of these issues and assume responsibility for our power to push the needle in the right direction, regardless of how daunting or distant the problem may feel.

You may have heard talk about the banana's extinction for about the past ten years. The beloved fruit consumed by so many of us throughout the world has been battling a deadly Panamanian disease, also known as banana wilt, which could be the end of the Cavendish variety that so many of us eat. If you think it can't happen, look at the 1950s example of the Gros Michel variety banana. Besides the disease, other factors like climate change, sustainability issues, and unfair business practices contribute to the potential fall of the banana.

You may think, "But what does this example have to do with me? What can I even do?" Do you want to live in a world without bananas? There may come a time when your children or grandchildren don't get to taste this amazing fruit. Do you want to be that person in the supermarket who feels disappointed because all the bananas are gone? (Don't even get us started on coffee.)

The sustainability of our planet relies on the actions of humans.

Humanity relies on the actions of individuals. We each make a difference, but the impact we make is so much greater when we work together. It's in the decisions we make, in how we consume, in how we travel, in how we work, in the amount of resources we use (think energy and water), and in the positive actions we take. We each have a role to play. This also ties into our previous skills of curiosity for deeper learning and trusting experts because, when the people who specialize in these issues tell us why they're important and how we can help, we need to listen.

Of course, many of the problems we listed are wicked problems; they are incredibly complex and might seem completely out of reach or daunting. The point of discussing these topics isn't to get caught in a doomsday scenario or depress others. It's to create awareness because we can do something. Consider the many ways that we, as consumers, can tackle global problems. We might purchase fair trade produce, for example. Our vote matters. We might investigate how representatives take action on issues like food security. Our work and jobs matter. Do we have a space in our work or personal lives to inspire others to take action?

Polarization can happen when we become consumed by issues that only we care about. It happens when we don't take responsibility for our actions and when we don't hold ourselves accountable for the contributions we make to the world. It also happens when we're too focused on individualism or on emotional pleas that make no real impact. When we recognize we're all in this together and work collectively, things will improve.

As educators, it's part of our job to help students discover how much they matter. We want them to internalize the notion that their decisions and actions impact others and our world in ways they might not even be able to fathom. We have a responsibility to each other to do our part. We never intended the word "freedom" to mean having a blatant disregard for others or harming others along the way. We must hold ourselves accountable for our actions and decisions. It not only makes us better people, but it also gives us a sense of purpose. Our actions matter, and collectively, we can do so much good.

CIVICS CONNECTION: OUR COLLECTIVE ACTIONS CHANGE THE WORLD

Wicked problems often cause students (and adults) to shut down. Let's stick with the banana example we just used. As soon as you explain the factors that influence this industry and the intricacies of the supply chain, people's eyes glaze over. The problem is so big and complex, so intangible, that it can leave people feeling disengaged and powerless.

But we get it. The glassy eyes result from a feeling of disconnect. Big problems feel out of our control. There are things we often cannot see or feel that make it difficult for us to understand our impact. These are the problems that are easy to avoid because we don't feel the repercussions of our inaction. It causes complacency.

We might better relate to other issues that get sensationalized. The closer a problem is to our lives, the more we feel a connection. For instance, a popular reality TV star is getting a divorce. Students who are avid viewers take on the situation as if it were their family. In another case, there was a clothing mishap at the Super Bowl, and everyone was up in arms the next day. It was all over social media and the news, but did it matter?

As civics teachers, we strive to ensure students can differentiate between pressing issues and distractions, but it can be hard when petty, often irrelevant stories dominate our media and our worries. We strive to make them understand (because this is the backbone of civic-mindedness) that their decisions, actions, and lifestyle choices have an impact, but we can only achieve this when they're able to understand what the world demands of them.

To hold ourselves accountable for the state of the world and its future, we must first help students understand what is important. We must create the connection and narrative that helps them connect with less appealing issues that actually impact the world. When students dig deeper into their understanding of the world, the demands will become clear. Once those demands are clear, we can help students realize their responsibility to do what they think is best—not just for themselves but for society, because that will improve their lives as well.

But it's hard when complacency is the norm and we do not promote community or society-based initiatives as helpful to individual pursuits. Take, for example, recycling. We all know that the whole recycling thing isn't working out as well as we'd like. Why is that? We believe it has everything to do with this disconnect we're discussing. People don't recycle or reduce their waste like they should in certain areas of the world because they truly don't see how it is benefiting them as individuals. A typical thought on the matter might be, *Why should I waste my time worrying about this when I don't see it having any positive and direct correlation in my life?* The lack of individual incentives regarding recycling or waste reduction has forced discussions on creative waste management, circular economies, and ensuring consumers produce less waste, such as plastics, as this pollution alone causes so much damage to our lands and waters.

When students understand the impacts of excessive waste and the harm plastics can do, it suddenly helps them realize the relevance behind recycling and waste reduction. Many coastal communities have seen the damage firsthand. Litter on beaches or plastic caught on marine life is often upsetting to those who witness these detrimental effects. The connection facilitates action and makes it easy to put bans on things like plastic bags. One of the greatest achievements we gain through collective leadership is policy change, and it's one of the reasons civics is so vital in helping students understand their power to generate impact.

Politics can help ease many of the issues happening in the world. In some places, politics and policies have become critical means of reducing waste and encouraging recycling. Having lived in both Switzerland and the United States, we can attest that the Swiss approach to dealing with waste is much more effective than in the US. Why? Because the Swiss are pragmatic. Citizens value the impact that comes with making policies and enforcing them. Specifically, the Swiss have implemented an initiative based on the "polluter pays" principle, in which consumers pay around $2 per trash bag, thus de-incentivizing their excessive use. The result has been a reduction in waste and an increase in recycling (around 20 percent) in the past two decades. While Switzerland still has a ways to go to reduce the waste it produces, this amazing initiative is a great example of the power of collective action. Maybe Americans could put more focus on this issue.

We have a responsibility not just to our nation and ourselves but to the world to move humanity forward. It's through our collective leadership that we will make progress. By understanding the issues, we can create shared goals to work toward. When students understand what these goals are, they can hold themselves accountable so they can evaluate if they are doing their part. It has become abundantly clear that we can make a much greater impact when there's a policy in place than when it's up to individual consumers to decide not to use them. This is because people rarely think about these issues, and we can change that.

The future is now. Our current actions create the world we will soon live in. We need to prioritize what we invest our time and money in and what we spend our discussions on because the impact of these decisions affects billions of people. Students are often happy to think beyond themselves; we just need to challenge them to do so.

If you're looking for a starting point on how to engage students on wicked problems where we need collective leadership, we advise you to engage them in the United Nations Sustainable Development Goals (SDGs).

MAKE THIS SKILL A REALITY

We like to run a simple exercise with students or have teachers run it with their students. We pass out slips of paper and ask each student to write down their definition of a changemaker. After they write the definition, we ask them if they feel like a changemaker based on the description they just wrote. Most students will say a changemaker is someone who makes a difference, and most students will firmly write that they are not a changemaker. It always feels a bit eye-opening because while we might see the potential and capacity of our students, it can be shocking when they don't recognize the obvious in themselves (we'll talk more about changemaking in Chapter 10).

Small actions matter. Sometimes students might not recognize the value of their contributions because they don't believe what they are doing is "big" enough. Too often, we, as a society, promote a sort of superhero world where we need to rely on one person to change everything. While it's great to have role models and to expose students to great leaders, expecting every person to walk in the footsteps of changemakers like Gandhi, Martin Luther King Jr., or Malala Yousafzai is a big ask. The pressure or expectation that students need to do something so grandiose can cause them to feel like failures.

To help students understand their power, we also need to normalize the small, everyday actions we can each perform to make the world a better place. Every person has a role to play in society, and we need to let students also know that while we would be super proud of them, it's okay if they don't achieve such widespread greatness. In the same way that we need scientists and doctors, we need custodians and trash collectors. We should value all people in our society and recognize the worth of every individual. Many roles that are the backbone of society, unfortunately, get little recognition. Students should never feel their worth is determined solely by their career but by how they treat others and how they lead their lives. When we take class time to recognize the little actions they take to support one another, their classroom, or their community, we help them realize that small actions do make a difference. As their confidence grows, we hope they will become bolder in their steps.

Collective leadership is about showing the power of unity. We don't need superheroes but rather a world where everyone understands they have value and power and that their contributions matter. When we all do those small actions together, it ends up making a big difference in the end, and that's where real change and transformation come from. This is why collective leadership matters in the classroom. Do your students feel like they have a voice and their actions matter? Do they internalize the notion that they have the power to act, no matter how small that action might be?

For us, the starting point to promoting collective leadership in the classroom is for students to understand their self-worth, the impact they make, and how they are a piece of the bigger whole. How we teach can reflect this. Students know that in some classes, everyone's on their own, looking out for their own learning and their own grade. In other classes, it feels like a community where students work together and learn from one another. Their grades often reflect how well they solve problems as a team. One format supports collective leadership over the other. Recognizing small actions and giving praise when students do things for others are the small steps we can take to help students understand the power of unity and collectivism.

Here are some of our ideas about how to advocate for our students to think with the greater good in mind and lay the foundation for collective leadership in the classroom.

STRATEGIES YOU CAN IMPLEMENT RIGHT AWAY

Idea #31: Use teamwork to build community and self-worth.

Make cooperation and teamwork a classroom priority. This is simple, but it gets to the point of advocating for the greater good. Encourage your students to work together as much as possible. Play games requiring teamwork. It's just a matter of being intentional. What can you think of that you regularly do that requires cooperation among your students? What activities do they do in the classroom that require teamwork? Whatever it is, emphasize it. Help your students understand the value of teamwork and the idea of being a part of something bigger than ourselves.

A simple way to get started with this is to ensure some assignments or assessments require teamwork. Take it a step further and allow time for them to debrief on the experience to reflect on what they learned.

How was the experience of working in a team? What did you learn about yourself? About others? What skills did you gain from the experience? What skills have room for improvement? Examples of skills might include:

- Actively listening to others
- Producing a high-quality product
- Being accountable
- Clear communication
- Active engagement or buy-in
- Playing off each other's strengths

Ask students to reflect on their growth and experience as team members throughout the year.

Idea #32: Develop awareness about impact.

It's hard to promote collective leadership if we aren't challenged to think about impact. Everything we do has an impact. Helping students to be aware of their impact can inspire them to be more intentional in their behavior and understand that their actions matter. An activity to engage students in impact is to have them assess their footprint and handprint. Often used in the environmental space, footprints focus on the negative impacts of our actions. Handprints focus on beneficial actions we can take. Both measurements can be useful, as they can help us understand how our actions generate an impact on the world.

Footprint: Here are a few examples to help students assess where they are and how, collectively, their actions add up:

- Encourage students to keep any plastic bottles they use during the week and bring them to class. See how many you have by the end of the week. Do the math. How many bottles did students use on average? Multiply that by the global population. Now, go deeper: What did you learn? What are the impacts of generating this amount of waste? Is recycling enough? What could we do to ease this problem?

- Ask students to count the number of trash bags their family uses in a week. Add it all up. Then have them investigate the number of trash bags people use per year in different countries. How did their family compare? What did they discover or conclude from their investigations?

Handprint: Here are a few examples to help students assess positive behavior. We like to emphasize the handprint because leaving students with only information on their footprint can sometimes disempower them and leave them with a sense of doom and gloom. The handprint demonstrates all the opportunities before us to take action.

- Remember the ALS ice-bucket challenge? It generated over $220 million worldwide. Challenge students to see how they might use social media as a force for good to generate funds for a good cause.

- Encourage students to go home and give a compliment to each member of their family. Have a debrief the next day to uncover the reactions.

- Help students create a community garden at school or host an event to plant trees. Have them assess the impact of their hard work over the year.

- Ask students to create their own handprint idea for a problem they care about.

Idea #33: Get to the root of the problems.

Collective leadership is not about saving others. It's about empowering one another while also holding ourselves accountable for our actions. Sometimes when we think about impact, we focus on those initiatives that make us feel good but don't solve the problem.

Here's an example: donating canned goods is a worthwhile experience. It can help students feel their power to act and do for others. The reality, however, is that canned donations do not address poverty. Often, when we get to the root cause of a problem, it inspires us to see the various pathways to action and the actors needed to fulfill those pathways. In this way, we can mull over a problem and how we might work together to solve it. So with that said, have students do a root cause analysis on a service-learning project or environmental or social issue. See what they uncover.

Idea #34: Play *Teenage World*.

We live in an interconnected world. Not only does each one of us have a role to play, but we also need each other for our society to function. Teenage World is a game that advocates teamwork and the need to work together for the common good. Here's how to get your students involved in this role-play activity:

Provide them with this prompt and then ask them to answer the following questions in groups:

> *Imagine that when you wake up tomorrow morning, all people over sixteen years of age have disappeared. There are no parents to tell you what to do, no teachers to educate the youth, no police officers to enforce the laws, and no government leaders to set policy. The military no longer exists, nor do the people who serve as doctors, nurses, paramedics, and firefighters. In short, adult authority and services have vanished. As teenagers, you are the oldest people in this new world. You have complete freedom of action, as well as new responsibilities.*

Part I

Answer the following questions to help you and your group think about what the foundation of your new society will be.

1. Decide which natural rights people should enjoy. (Keep in mind that natural rights are not determined by the government; they simply stem from the fact that you are human. Example: A natural right may be to travel freely but not to travel fast and dangerously. A government may step in to make free travel safer.)

2. Consider your interactions with others. What two to four problems might arise in your new society if everyone has complete freedom of action?

3. As an individual, are you capable of securing all the natural rights you have listed in number one? If yes, how? If no, why not?

4. Are there areas in which you would need to cooperate with others? If no, why? If yes, give two to four examples.

5. Are there common concerns you should address together in your society (areas that aren't needs, but it would be nice if people worked together to make things happen)?

Part II

Answer the following questions as if everyone in our society has the human nature of either being a pessimist or an optimist (assign your students to one or the other).

1. Do you have an obligation to help the less capable members of society, such as young children? Feeble teens? Why or why not?

2. Do you think that disputes (about someone's rights being violated) will often or rarely arise between members of your society? How do you think you should solve them? Why?

3. To carry out its decisions, how powerful (in enforcing and punishing) do you think the government needs to be? Why?

4. Should the people have a voice, direct or indirect, in determining the decisions of the government? Explain your answer.

5. Your society has common concerns, so you should think about a structure to address them. This means creating a government. In your society, how would you select the leaders of your government? (Should everyone, including your five-year-old sibling, have a voice in the selection process?) Explain your answer.

Idea #35: Encourage systems thinking through interdisciplinary activities.

Few issues in the world require only one skill or one discipline to effectively engage in the issue. It's interesting that we still teach subjects in silos when the disciplines work interdependently to equip students to take action. For this reason, we invite you to see if you can develop at least one interdisciplinary theme a year with colleagues.

Themes help students connect content and see how we weave together skills from various subject areas to take action. Thematic questions could be:

- What's a hero?

- How might we take climate action?

- How do we build community?

Subject-area teachers can each decide how they will use the theme to integrate content and standards. Working together, you will create a united front to show how learning is interwoven and how interconnected the subjects are.

CHAPTER 8

FIGHT APATHY AND PROMOTE EMPATHY

Encourage students to think and feel from multiple perspectives through empathy

The greatest danger to our future is apathy.
— JANE GOODALL

Essential Question: How do we encourage students to care?

Objective: Help students realize it is critical to learn how people around the world think, behave, and live with each other. The more our students learn how to think beyond their own scope, the better.

THE PROBLEM: STUDENTS DISPLAY APATHY ABOUT THE NEEDS AND FEELINGS OF OTHERS

MANY YEARS AGO, I (Michelle) was teaching a high school psychology course on the five senses. On a field trip, we ventured up to a city with a restaurant called the Blinde Kuh (Blind Cow). What makes this restaurant unique is that it functions in pure darkness. Most of the waitstaff are blind and therefore unaffected by the lack of lighting. However, for the clientele, the experience is a jolting reality of just how much we depend on our eyesight. Although the sentiments and realizations are different for each person, the restaurant proves to be an exercise in empathy. My students, though only getting a small taste of what it might be like to live with a disability, were not only able to put themselves into someone else's shoes, but they also could learn more about themselves and their biases.

Many students commented on the amount of work it took to simply find their utensils in the darkness and properly put food on their forks or spoons. Others noticed how little they could recognize tastes without seeing their food. Still others were weighed down by the hardships of having to learn to adapt to a life without sight; they had never imagined the difficulties. Others sat in admiration of the waitstaff for being able to do everything with such ease and grace, clearly not victims of their disability. I even noticed little things. I found it difficult to speak, as I rely so much on facial expressions and cues to guide me in conversation. It's also a reason I'm quite bad at social media, but I digress.

We believe another contributing factor to the polarization we see in our societies is an overwhelming sense of apathy toward one another. People often don't seem bothered enough to get involved in issues that don't directly impact them, and many give the impression that they just do not care about what is happening beyond their own bubble. It's as if we've lost our curiosity, not just toward learning about new subjects but also about how problems impact peoples' lives. We forget that the faces of those who bear the burden of some of the greatest hardships we see on the news (e.g., poverty or war) are indeed human faces with needs similar to our own. We understand that we as individuals can't solve every problem out there, but to dismiss them seems unfair.

There's a sign I (Michelle) saw hanging from a window of a residence close to where I live. It read, "If you're not angry, you're not paying attention." It's not the first time I've seen the expression, but this phrase always strikes different emotions in me. On the one hand, it's good to be aware of what's happening in the world and to feel empowered to do something. On the other hand, anger often causes people to act irrationally. Shouting matches, blame, and shame do not create progress. To me, our anger causes us to take sides, to find an enemy on whom we can unleash our anger.

We need people to care but in a thoughtful way. In a highly globalized world, we should be aware of what is happening across the globe and how issues impact others. We can't expect our students to take action, to be good citizens, if they don't care about what's going on around them. It's in learning to value the feelings and experiences of others that we can motivate our students to be kinder and more understanding of one another. When we learn to care, we're encouraged to let go of our complacency and, ultimately, take action to make things better.

THE SOLUTION: FIGHT APATHY AND PROMOTE EMPATHY

Empathy is about thinking differently and deeply about the experiences and viewpoints of others so your knowledge of the world grows. In learning about and internalizing these emotions and feelings, we learn more about ourselves as well. This skill, this ability to put oneself in the shoes of another, is beneficial in many ways. It enables us to treat others the way they want to be treated. We're much less likely to engage others in constructive dialogue if we neglect their needs, feelings, and experiences. If we never learn to look beyond our own viewpoint, or we dismiss the voices of others, then we cannot expect to find a middle ground. Empathy is what can help us find the thread that unites us.

> *Those who can find a way out of a narrow or simplistic perspective can broaden their understanding of others and develop empathy, reducing polarization.*

We are all human. If we look at Maslow's hierarchy of needs, we see humans are the same on all levels. For example, we all need love for family and friends and a sense of belonging. These threads transcend us all. It's usually the perceived differences that divide us.

Empathy is a critical ingredient for preventing polarization. Of course, teaching empathy is difficult. How do you create situations where students can truly feel the experiences of others? Talking is often insufficient, and imagining is a good place to start, but putting yourself into someone else's place is often best when experiencing their world for yourself.

Mark Twain said, "Travel is fatal to prejudice, bigotry, and narrow-mindedness, and many of our people need it sorely on these accounts. Broad, wholesome, charitable views of men and things cannot be acquired by vegetating in one little corner of the earth all one's lifetime."

Individuals who are limited to their own experiences and are confined to their own communities might find it difficult to have a sense of the behavior, thoughts, and motivations of those living beyond their communities. This, of course, is a problem. People limited by a narrow existence and simplistic viewpoints on issues make themselves vulnerable to becoming polarized. This is a problem that continues to worsen, not only in our country but also in many countries around the world.

Conversely and optimistically, those who can find a way out of a narrow or simplistic perspective can broaden their understanding of others and develop empathy, reducing polarization. Travel is a wonderful way to develop empathy, but we know not everyone can hop on a plane and see a new part of the world. We get it. There are financial and time considerations. Fortunately, technology allows us—now more than ever—to "travel" anywhere in the world anytime we want. Books, music, art, and film all provide lenses into the world of others. Developing empathy doesn't have to mean seeking different cultures and experiences. Honestly, we can home in on the experience component and develop empathy well within our own communities and schools. Gaining empathy might be as simple as talking to that person whom others ignore. It may be ensuring our students love themselves.

Sometimes students might use apathy to mask insecurities, self-doubt, or dissatisfaction with their lives. As educators, our first step might be to introduce our students to self-empathy, a practice where we encourage individuals to embrace their experiences and feelings and try to understand themselves. Regardless of where students begin, it's important that we do something to start their journey of caring. Without that, we can't expect them to bother. If they feel nothing, why would they act?

CIVICS CONNECTION: BUILD EMPATHY BY UNDERSTANDING MOTIVATION

Empathy. Inclusion. Knowing what's happening in other parts of the world. These should be key ingredients that all social studies teachers include in their classrooms, particularly civics teachers. The more we learn how to think and experience beyond our scope, the better. You could make the argument that instilling this section's skill—building empathy—is the base skill in breaking down the barriers that cause polarization. Twain's quote rings true: learning about others and seeking an understanding of who they are strips away feelings that lead to disconnection and even bigoted behaviors.

Many emotions arise in civics class. It may bring to light that many policies are driven by fear (we use this word loosely). People might fear change. They might fear for their livelihood or safety. They might fear getting overlooked and ignored. To help people understand why a group votes a certain way, we might find it necessary to investigate why they feel that fear. For example, why vote in favor of coal if renewables are proving to be more profitable (and cleaner!) than fossil fuels? Well, if you know that an area has been dependent upon coal jobs for generations, it makes it much easier to understand their concerns and motivations.

Another emotion explored in civics is belonging. If you feel you don't belong and the system doesn't support you, why would you bother engaging? The United States has been known to be biased in how it portrays its history and who gets represented (look at a sampling of history textbooks, and this is usually not too difficult to verify). We also have high levels of inequality (take a look at our latest score on the Gini Index) coupled with a subpar social safety net compared to other developed countries. Our point is that many feel like their tax money or government doesn't do much for their personal well-being, so why should they engage?

Feelings and sentiments motivate much of our behavior (perhaps most). To understand why people believe what they do, we must be able to understand their emotions and viewpoints and the experiences that have led them to these conclusions.

Too often in civics class, we might dismiss people as stupid or misguided without truly understanding their journey and what led them to their conclusions. If we want to move forward on issues, we must understand the "why" behind people's motives and behaviors. Of course, this is more easily done when students have empathy. Like in the other chapters of this book, this is a skill that's nearly impossible to develop overnight, which is why we hope all teachers work toward equipping their students with this invaluable skill.

MAKE THIS SKILL A REALITY

Society is pushing for more social and emotional learning (SEL) in the classroom, and we love it. We believe it lays the groundwork for many other skills. As teachers, we have all struggled with a student or group of students who just doesn't seem to care. Sometimes it's hard to care about others if your own needs aren't being met. A first step toward preventing apathy is ensuring students feel valued and loved.

If you want to get started on empathy work, here are some basic actions you can take. First, start with self-empathy. Empathy takes a level of confidence and self-love before we can engage with the thoughts and feelings of others. Many of our young people just want to be seen. Actively listen to your students and pay attention to what is happening in their lives. It's normal for young people to not always be able to think beyond their own existence, their own bubble (especially in their teen years). Help them notice what is happening in the world and in their communities. As educators, we have ample opportunities to let our students know they're cared for and to help them learn to love themselves. When they practice these basics, it opens the doorway for them to pass on the good vibes and extend their care and concern for others as well. Below are some of our favorite ideas to help them flex their empathy skills.

STRATEGIES YOU CAN IMPLEMENT RIGHT AWAY

Idea #36: Do the *Bucket Check* activity.

We can't expect students to care or empathize with others if they don't feel good about themselves. It can be hard to discuss these topics with students, which is why we suggest putting easy-to-use language around the issue. A popular book titled *How Full Is Your Bucket?* has versions for children and adults. It provides young people with a way to gauge how they're feeling and what made them feel that way. Based on the age level of your students, it may be worthwhile to read the book with them and do an activity so they can assess their own bucket. For older students, we recommend familiarizing them with the concept and doing a journal entry on the topic.

Questions might include:

- How full is your bucket?
- What makes your bucket feel full?
- What makes your bucket feel empty?
- What do you do to fill other people's buckets?
- What might you stop doing that dips from other people's buckets?

Once students are familiar with the concept, they will have a shared language to express when they're not feeling okay in a less personal and more approachable manner.

Idea #37: Develop empathy through the arts.

Many creative works offer us an opportunity to engage in the world through a different lens. Artists give us a piece of themselves through their work. Help students understand how they might use those outlets to see the world through someone else's eyes.

Photography and art

Help students find empathy through art. Photography offers a unique entry point, as we're stuck in the juxtaposition of seeing what the photo captures and wondering about the motivation of the person behind the lens. As a society, we often get so bombarded with images that they lose their power to spark feelings or actions. Pick a photo for your class that made an impact on society (e.g., sparked protests, an uproar in society, or a political response). These photos might be shocking and spark an array of emotions, so be sure they are age-appropriate. Although it's a deep and emotional task, ask students to describe what they learned from engaging with these pictures. Questions may include:

- What does the picture show?
- What does the picture make you feel?
- Would you have wanted this picture taken if you were related to the person in the photograph? Explain.
- Should someone have taken this picture? Is it ethical for people to take these types of photos?
- What do you think the camera operator felt?
- Why do you believe this photo sparked action?

Books and films

Books and films don't always teach empathy. We must facilitate the questions that help students pause, internalize, and feel the perspectives of others. Books offer us a lens into how authors view the world. Make sure your classroom library offers a wide range of literature with authors from different countries and cultures that can expose students to a diverse range of perspectives. Provide guided questions or conversations with students so they can learn to reflect on what they are reading and engage with the questions these pieces of literature provide.

Films can offer the same insights as books, but again, it's a matter of hosting a platform to digest insights, spark debate, and offer critiques. Foreign films can give us insights into other cultures. Provocative series like *The Wire* can help us explore our own systems.

Comparing books to films can lend itself to character studies, which is an excellent way to help students learn empathy.

If you've only watched *Les Misérables*, you can't help but dislike Inspector Javert for his insatiable quest to capture our hero, Jean Valjean. If you've read the book, however, you begin to understand that Inspector Javert is not necessarily the evil villain we see in the films but perhaps a man who deeply holds to his own ethical code, a person guided by his values to uphold the law to the utmost degree.

Encourage students to do the same with literature they like. What do students learn from key characters in books like *The Hunger Games*, *Harry Potter*, or *The Hate U Give* that they wouldn't have uncovered if they had only watched the film?

Idea #38: Practice a language with a native speaker.

Encourage students to apply their language skills beyond the classroom. Assign them to practice speaking a new language with a native speaker. Having lived in multiple countries, we speak from experience when we say it is humbling to attempt to speak a foreign language and to not be able to communicate your needs. Have students write a journal entry about the experience.

Here are some prompts:

- How did it feel to converse in a new language with a native speaker?

- Did you feel like yourself when speaking?

- How do you think it would feel to fully immerse yourself in this new language and not be able to use your native tongue?

- Did this experience change how you feel about others who are working on learning a new language?

Idea #39: Follow the *Platinum Rule*.

Let's go beyond the Golden Rule. To help our students listen, ask, and observe, we suggest exposing students to the Platinum Rule. The Platinum Rule moves from "Do unto others as you would have done unto you" and progresses the concept to "Do unto others as they would want you to do to them."

It's an important difference. For example, how do we provide recognition for a job well done? A thank-you note might please Person A, while Person B might want a celebratory party. If each had applied the Golden Rule, it would have disappointed the other person. Person A might feel embarrassed by being the center of attention, and Person B might be disappointed by such a small gesture. We can't assume people would want us to do what we would like others to do for us.

Here are two quick activities to engage others in the Platinum Rule:

- Find a place to display the Platinum Rule on a poster in your room. Make it a visual focal point for your students.

- Ask students what the difference between the Golden Rule and Platinum Rule means to them. Let the discussion flow openly.

Idea #40: Play the *Common Sense* activity.

Too often, we assume others know what we know. We can be quick to shame others for not having common sense. As educators, we know that making assumptions about what people are knowledgeable about doesn't get us anywhere. Our backgrounds and experiences vary widely, giving each of us a different breadth of knowledge. This idea helps us get a more holistic view and ditch this notion of universal common sense.

The *Common Sense* activity:

Ask your students to write down an example of a topic they view as common sense.

In groups of two to three, have them share their lists with each other.

- How were their lists similar?

- How were they different?

- What makes them believe something should be common sense?

- Were there items on other people's lists that they did not believe were common sense? Why?

The goal here is to get the kids to realize that common sense is an illusion. For example, a student might say that it's common sense to drive on the right side of the road. Well, not if they are living in the UK. You're preparing pasta. What do you add to the boiling water as it cooks? Some might point out that it's common sense to add a little salt and oil. The list can go on and on. See what your students feel is common sense and if they still feel that way after this activity.

CHAPTER 9

ENGAGE IN MORAL AMBIGUITY

Ditch the good guy versus bad guy outlook

I've yet to meet a person in my life who doesn't have some moral ambiguity.

— JASON BEGHE

Essential Question: How can we help students understand the value and impact their character has on their decisions?

Objective: Enable students to see the connections between their ethics and morals and the decisions they make.

THE PROBLEM: WE AREN'T CHALLENGED TO THINK DEEPLY ABOUT OUR VALUES AND HOW WE LIVE THEM

AMERICANS LOVE A happy ending. A common critique from outside observers is that American films show that we want to live in a world where the "good guy" wins. Other cultures have questioned why we go for this ideal over the more probable reality that things will not work out. The answer is simple: it's because we like justice and admire people who are good-hearted and honorable and stand for what's right. Film-makers know their market. As Americans, we can't stand the person who rises to the top by taking advantage of the "little guy." We detest that person who is cutthroat and only out for themselves, no matter how outwardly successful they might become. We like to imagine we live in a just world that rewards fairness and decency, so for us, the bad guy can't be the winner. We'd exit the movie theater outraged and irritated.

Of course, films rarely reflect reality. Character, ethics, and morals are trickier than we might give them credit for. We don't live in a world of good guys and bad guys where the right choice is obvious or easy. Most people do not dress as villains with a clear agenda to violently destroy lives and property like we see in the comics or in movies. Actions that might have devastating impacts come in much more subtle packages and are often taken by people who look like Mom or Pop (and who may even have the best of intentions). Therefore, it's important we not only look deeply at issues but also ensure we rely on our moral compass and ethical code to help us make the best decisions possible.

That's precisely what makes this chapter so interesting and important. Do our choices in how we vote, the policies we support, and how we engage with others truly represent the values we claim to have? As a society, we rarely get to reflect on our values and assess if we are living our ideals (or at least trying to). It often takes a lot of work to truly live by our morals and ethics. But talking about them and living them are two separate things. In such a complex world, how do we help young people navigate their morals and abide by their ethics? How do we lay the groundwork for living, working, and voting on what we say we value? How do we help students understand that many issues cause moral dilemmas, and it's not necessarily "evil people" causing bad things to happen but rather the repercussions of dealing with multifaceted problems? Having the opportunity to reflect on the decisions we make and their impact, in relationship to the values we wish to adhere to, should be a simple tenet of good citizenship and a way to gauge how we are doing as a society.

This led us to explore how people learn about character and the outlets through which they might explore their morality and ethical code. Of course, we get to wrestle with these decisions through daily occurrences. Our interactions with peers, family, or friends may demonstrate to us that we value traits like loyalty, openness, or kindness. Think of those you respect and who energize you; what traits do you admire? Current events, literature, and film are just a few of the mediums through which we get exposed to dilemmas that might shine a light on our own set of values. Think of the reactions to popular films, books, or series like *Don't Look Up*, *The Handmaid's Tale*, or *How to Be an Antiracist*. Where did you stand? As much as we get exposed to opportunities to engage in discussions around morals, ethics, and values, how often do people take the opportunity to reflect on their actions and choices in relation to them?

What's measured gets improved. It's important that we encourage young people to grapple with these issues and set a standard for the type of world they want to live in. Especially in our youth, we're built to learn from mistakes and grow, not just literally but figuratively, into the types of people we want to be. This is why it's so important to talk about and nurture topics on character and morality. It's the only way to ensure we equip young people to walk the talk and strengthen that inner voice that tells them when something is not right. It is yet another opportunity to help them uncover what they care about and the issues they feel matter most.

THE SOLUTION: ENGAGE IN MORAL AMBIGUITY

Polarization can happen when we fail to equip our youth with guidance on morality, ethics, and character. When schools fail to provide an outlet through which students can explore these topics, it can have negative repercussions. Students turn into adults who are ill-equipped to explore the ambiguity that comes with solving tough problems. They might cling to superficial views that are validating and easier to digest than reality. As an economics teacher, I (Michelle) have had students dismiss issues like poverty with justifications like "People are poor because they're lazy." I've stopped lessons cold to address that fallacy and focus on the importance of policies to strengthen the workforce and improve the quality of life, as well as the reality that jobs that require "hard work" don't necessarily pay well. Without someone to help them explore these issues, we are leaving them to their own devices. Often, they turn to religious organizations or to the media for a sense of guidance. This can be polarizing on both fronts.

> *If we learn how to embrace moral ambiguity, then we can learn how to treat people decently as we work to find consensus on complicated issues.*

As we have discussed before, media—all of it, including films, television, news, blogs, and social media—can polarize, as they tend to sensationalize situations and oversimplify issues. When this happens, people can unknowingly put themselves into moral camps based on who they feel are the "good guys." Issues are usually complex and beyond our comprehension or the effort we put into understanding the intricacies of a situation. It can be damaging to label the other side as "bad" or "evil" when it's often not so simple. If we dig deeper, we might find that we're in a moral dilemma where there are no right answers.

Consider the idea of abortion. In one camp, people firmly believe they are saving the lives of innocent children. In the other camp, people are protecting the rights and lives of women. No matter how flawed or short-sighted you may feel the other side's views are, most people do not approach the issue with bad intentions. When we can remove hatred and lower the emotional response, we're more likely to understand the motivations of others and have a constructive dialogue.

Another example of a dilemma might come from evaluating the effectiveness of an idea. Sometimes, we're in a situation where an idea might be worthwhile but implemented poorly. Standardized testing comes to mind. In the education space, we might view proponents of standardized testing negatively while we view those against standardized testing in a more positive light. Modern standardized tests in the US were mandated with the goal of closing the achievement gap. Most educators would agree that closing the achievement gap is important. It's the implementation of how to achieve this goal that we need to rethink, and we need to work together to do that effectively. Again, when we move away from the good guy versus bad guy mentality, we can have a more productive chat on how to achieve our goals.

Making things easy to assimilate, no matter how inaccurate, can cause people to feel validated in their beliefs and their way of life and feel as if they have a superior moral and ethical code. Memes on social media validate an emotion and make us feel we're good, even if they dramatically oversimplify a situation. Clichés in films might not represent reality. How many times have you seen a film where a successful corporate executive from the city comes to the countryside, only to find rebirth through exposure to the simple life? What if the corporate executive helped transform the economy of a dying town into something more profitable and sustainable? Why the negative connotation when we know nothing about that person or the quality of the initiative underway?

Too often, we have a superficial view of the character of other groups, and it can cause us to be unkind. We usually choose what we consume, making us more likely to engage with media that doesn't push our thinking or help us understand the ethical and moral implications of our choices. When we take sides based on a superficial understanding of what's going on, it makes it easier to have an opinion but can cause us to be more reactive than necessary.

If we learn how to embrace moral ambiguity, then we can learn how to treat people decently as we work to find consensus on complicated issues. It can be hard for students to move beyond clichés that are so readily available when they consume media, especially if they don't have an outlet to truly reflect on and question the information and stories they're exposed to.

Religious institutions can also be polarizing, especially when they teach their followers that they have a monopoly on values and are superior to those outside of their organization. We are not attacking religion, but there is a reason most governments strive for a clear distinction between church and state. When one specific faith or religious organization yields too much power or influence in a certain country, it can create an unnecessary "us versus them" mentality that is counterproductive to open dialogue. What makes religion complicated is that people blur their ethics and morals into religious teachings, as if their religion is the only outlet through which one might learn to be a good person.

You can be a good person regardless of your religion. Honesty, kindness, respectfulness, and fairness are examples of character traits most humans admire. Humanity is united in its quest for love, connection, and meaning. Anywhere you go in the world, people will say they value things like family or education. We usually admire a person who exhibits traits like caring and fairness. No religion has a monopoly on doing good, on character, or on morality. This is why it's so critical to have a neutral space to get a better understanding of ourselves and others. More unites us than we might think.

So why do we take that risk of omitting conversations and opportunities to learn about who we are on the inside? Given how much the world needs good people, we shouldn't be afraid to discuss character, morality, or ethics in our schools, and we have ample opportunities to do so. The world especially needs good leaders, and there is nothing wrong with encouraging students to be upstanding citizens by showing them how to explore their ethics and values. Being a good person has nothing to do with the person's religion and everything to do with their actions and words and how they treat others. By omitting this dialogue, we do more harm than good by forcing people to navigate complicated situations alone. Even worse, they might not have the skills to break down complicated issues, so they become more prone to the manipulation of others.

We need people who can think for themselves and who have the moral courage to guide them. Let's strive for a world in which everyone is kind and tries to live and work as ethically as possible. Good character is a critical foundation for moving society forward. Your morals and ethics will act as drivers for how you want to shape your world and your community. One thing we can do to encourage the next generation to get involved in leadership positions is to stop perpetuating the stereotype that all politicians are corrupt.

Most students are ready to do more. They strive for purpose and meaning in what they learn and what they do. In a period in their lives when they're learning who they are, we don't need to tell them what to think. We need to give them the opportunity to dig deeper into their own sense of right and wrong. We need to prepare them to handle the complexity and ambiguity that come with the overwhelming realization of just how complex issues are. If not us, then who? Where else will students have the opportunity to question the world and their own character? The deeper we get into an issue, the more complicated it becomes and the more at a loss we feel on how to choose the best path forward. But that's okay. If we're preparing our youth to think about and do what's right—no matter how difficult—we'll get to where we're supposed to go.

CIVICS CONNECTION: TO WHAT DEGREE ARE CHURCH AND STATE SEPARATED?

Politics often has the reputation of being dirty or corrupt. Some educators try to steer kids away from pursuing it, saying it's only for power-hungry people with poor values. We believe that it's disturbing this narrative exists, as we're almost contributing toward a self-fulfilling prophecy of having poor leaders. Since everything is political, do we not want to create a society where we emphasize good character and values so we make good decisions? We need to change that discourse by making sure good character is a natural part of being a good citizen, a good leader, and one who makes good decisions. We should make being a politician an honorable job so we can motivate more of the good ones to take on the challenge.

Unfortunately, in the civics classroom, this negative stereotype is common. Not only is there a distrust of politics and politicians, but there is often a gap between what students say they value and the parties or policies they are for or against. When we move more deeply into issues, it forces them to question themselves and dig deeper into their belief systems. You can see them buckling under the weight of their moral compass and ethical code, especially when it doesn't align with what they've been told (e.g., labeling those in poverty as lazy). It's wondrous when this happens because it exemplifies the importance of understanding your inner voice, of having a conscience.

Most bigger decisions, especially at the policy level, are hard decisions. We are often stuck deciding on an option or plan that helps the most or harms the least. It's not easy, but it's reality. We might give students a scenario such as this: Five citizens are stuck in a storm. You need a rescue team of ten to save them. The conditions are dangerous, and the odds of surviving the mission are low. Do you still send your rescue team? Students will have varying answers as they grapple with choosing the right thing to do.

From there, we may take it a step further and relate the scenario to sending in troops to resolve a situation. Students begin to see just how complicated it can be to take action (or not). As good citizens, we need the type of people who can have tough conversations, entertain thoughts they might not agree with, and be brave through the ambiguity. The world has a lot of problems, and we need people who can think critically and compassionately about them to suggest solutions.

This creates an even more interesting situation in the civics classroom when we pretend our belief systems shape the policies for which we advocate. This pushes on the idea that in the United States, we have a true separation between church and state. But do we? The reality we are trying to express here is that there is a distinct association between religion and politics. As we have alluded to throughout this book, there is a connection between institutions and politics, so why would religion stay clear of political inclinations?

As we explore and dig deeper, students understand just how many dilemmas exist. The more we dive into ethical dilemmas (choosing between two morally sound options), the more we understand how complicated and interconnected the world is and why making the right choice is never as simple as it seems. Of course, the easiest way to teach and expose students to these types of dilemmas is through the very outlets that can polarize—media and religion. Often, we're given the green light to teach about media and media consumption (although in many places, we could still use more support and trust in the teaching of current events), but we're told to avoid social media and religion at all costs.

It is difficult to teach social studies without teaching about religions. People, cultures, and places are so heavily influenced by their belief systems that it's mind-blowing that we are expected to teach about the world and its histories without tapping into this critical institution and motivator that drives both systems and behavior. We can't avoid teaching about religions. When we talk about religions, we show how united humanity is. We just can't advocate one religion over another in a public setting.

Teaching ancient world religions has taught us that values all over the world are largely the same. (Or ethics or morals are largely the same.) Whether it be the Bible, the Quran, Greek mythology, or Aesop's Fables—these all explore life lessons on morality. Rituals, customs, and creation stories might be different, but most religions are in complete accordance with what is right and wrong.

Is there a religious doctrine that advocates for hatred, intolerance, the planet's exploitation, greed, or corruption? Is there a doctrine that promotes treating people unfairly or cruelly? The world needs people who have good characters who can engender a world where everyone treats everyone respectfully, where everyone does their work as ethically as possible, and where good leaders rule and make good decisions. The fear, however, is that educators will not cover the topic objectively. Therefore, instead of addressing the obvious, we try to avoid the topic at all costs. This is problematic for several reasons.

- It can promote ignorance or misunderstanding. We assume that other religions do not promote the same moral principles because we confuse their customs and rituals for ethics.

- It can prevent critical thinking. What do your ideals look like from a policy standpoint? Is that what's happening? You need more than one outlet to assess and evaluate your beliefs.

- It can promote bigotry. Religious organizations often put their religion on a pedestal, which may cause intolerance toward other groups. Learning about different religions can demonstrate what we have in common instead of focusing on what divides us.

- It can minimize accountability. Is it up to God (or some other supreme being), or can *you* contribute? Our character makes us accountable for our actions and contributes to our sense of responsibility to do for others. Why would we leave that up to religious leaders?

When we discuss religion, it can help students think critically about how much we might cling to superficial arguments, clichés, and unvalidated beliefs. Uncomfortable feelings might surface, but it's important to give students a space to reflect on their own worldview. Despite what we just discussed, there is still a division between church and state. The point of our comments is that this doesn't mean that people don't vote based on their values, their ethics, or their morals. The point of our comments is that, without a deeper look, there appears to be hypocrisy, cognitive dissonance, and complacency in what we say we value and the policies we put in place. When students make the connection between their belief system, their sense of right and wrong, how they live, and what they vote for, then we can truly make progress.

MAKE THIS SKILL A REALITY

In the civics classroom, students can discuss what's right and wrong. They're shocked to learn that most issues are incredibly complicated and there are many gray areas. As you discuss key issues, you can see students battle internally with what the right thing to do is. They realize many decisions are hard, but it's by examining their ethics and values, by understanding the needs of people, that they can make the best choices. Some of their choices highlight just who those students truly are on the inside.

Providing a space to make choices and reflect on them is a great way for students to understand their ethics and values. In the classroom, there are multiple ways to incorporate character. It's in the content (in literature, we analyze a character and the choices they make; in science, we ask what science should advance) or how we treat and work with each other. We can provide an outlet for students to explore their morality, their conscience, and their actions.

Social and emotional learning has created a foundation for which we can help students further develop their character and embrace moral ambiguity. We have noticed an uptick in books and programs for little ones that emphasize traits like kindness, respect, or caring, but it seems to fizzle out as we go through elementary school. This is a shame, as that's also when life gets more complicated for most. We wonder how we can keep that momentum going so students understand how to self-regulate and manage their emotions and behaviors, which are critical to their success when working with others who may not think like them.

We often steer away from philosophy in K–12, but getting a little philosophical is the best way to help students think differently and deeply about their world. Critical thinking comes into play when students must work through an ethical dilemma, one where there's no right answer, and this is truly exquisite. Try this one: Ask students if it's ever okay to lie or if it's ever okay to break a rule. It's humbling to know that there are multiple ways to view a problem, and every single viewpoint can be morally sound. Giving students the opportunity to think through ethical or moral dilemmas or to assess their decisions and the impact of those decisions gives them the foundation to deal with ambiguity, make difficult choices, and follow their moral compass.

Whether it's embedded in the content through daily interactions or in how we handle behavior issues and classroom management, students need a chance to grow as people. Let's work to provide that chance for our students. Let's push ourselves to provide the space, environment, and skills necessary for students to understand the importance of moral and ethical behavior in our governments and societies. And let's give them the guidance they need to come to terms with what morality and ethics mean to them.

STRATEGIES YOU CAN IMPLEMENT RIGHT AWAY

Idea #41: Reward awesomeness with *Character in the Classroom.*

How are we reinforcing the good qualities students exhibit? As we have mentioned, promoting and understanding social and emotional learning is a vital piece of building character in the classroom. As teachers, we need to remind ourselves how crucial it is to praise student behaviors that help instill the basic elements of social and emotional learning, such as kindness, gratitude, empathy, and altruism. We can concretely instill the idea of character building within our students. Here are a few ways:

1. Have students create a student campaign targeted toward a particular issue in need of awareness or support. (Again, we can think of the ALS Ice-Bucket

Challenge from a few years ago.) Have them use social media, if possible. Let their creativity emerge.

2. Develop star charts. Reward good character in your students with a simple sticker by a student's name when they do something awesome. This one is old school, but it's still effective at certain age levels. We all love being praised.

3. Role model a role-playing activity: Have your students do research on an individual they feel is a powerful example of someone who displays a strong and virtuous character. Ask the students to create a script where they play this person and highlight their good deeds within the role-play.

Idea #42: Let students embrace negative emotions.

Too often in school, we discourage negativity. We ask kids to tell us about their passions or what they love, but guess what? A lot of them don't know. Don't feel obligated to use positivity to get kids to express what matters to them. We've found that letting kids tap into their anger and frustrations has been a far more fruitful way to help them articulate what they care about. Once they know what bothers them, use sense-making to help them explore the issue. Why is that issue happening? What factors come into play? Encourage them to dig deeper into their understanding of things. This will equip them with the insights they need to act.

Here are three basic steps to help you out:

Step 1: Be a supporter of angry children. Our upbringing has trained us to suppress anger, but anger is a driver and a motivator for action. Of course, we're not encouraging a bunch of angry, screaming kids to riot in your classroom, but we are encouraging you to ask what bothers them. Help them recognize that anger is because they feel an injustice. Their minds and guts tell them what they think is immoral or unethical. Help them figure out why they feel that anger. Help them have a constructive dialogue. Then help them figure out what they can do to address it.

Step 2: Give them a simple prompt to get started. Ask students to think about what bothers them. Give them the opportunity to rattle off all those things they feel in the pit of their stomachs that are unjust. Then, present them with situations or topics that might make them uncomfortable or stir a reaction. Ask them how they feel about each item that's presented. Help students recognize that their feelings, and their body's response, are a great way for them to identify what they care about.

Step 3: Help them funnel that anger. Emphasize that anger is sometimes associated with caring, and that's okay, but it's important to develop positive outlets to move forward. For example, if seeing litter on the side of the road makes a student angry, help them see it's their mind's way of telling them this is an issue that is important to them, and it is a sign that this would be a good activity to act on. Have them dig deeper into the topic: Why do people litter? How could we change that behavior? Could we organize a clean-up?

This is the purpose of politics: to provide a space for citizens to address the issues we care about and to design the world we want to live in. Unfortunately, this notion has been removed from most people's views. Many people don't make the connection between anger and caring, and they might lash out in unconstructive ways. So many people are just angry, and they don't know what to do with that anger. If people have never been taught to recognize it for what it is (caring) or learned to develop strategies for doing something positive and proactive with that anger, it can have damaging effects on that person's well-being and on how they interact with others.

Idea #43: Role-play *What Would You Do?* dilemma debates.

All ages can do this if you make adjustments based on maturity. This idea is similar to the role-play discussed above, but instead of promoting acting out, it encourages students to engage in actual debates with others. For example, ask the students to provide their views (either as truly their own views or by assigning a point of view) by going back and forth on the different stances on certain issues. And these issues can be big, important, and even controversial, depending on the age of your students. Debate on issues like: Should we endorse corporal punishment in schools? Can the government ban donuts? Should assisted suicide be legal in some instances? Know your audience to ensure they can handle the topic.

This could even be an activity based on the popular television show *What Would You Do?* Provide a scenario to your students that is complicated and has a bit of a gray area to it. Give the students time to decide how they would respond to the situation and what factors they base it on.

Another way to promote the idea of ethical dilemma is to engage your students in a game we created called The Gray Zone. You can find this game on our website, civicsthroughplay.com. Through this exercise, students practice their critical thinking and communication skills while empathizing with ideas they may not agree with. The goal of this game is to get students to understand that there's not always a clear right or wrong and to think about their own morals and ethics.

Here's how to play The Gray Zone:

1. Pass out cards that deal with various "gray" topics. Visit the website or create your own. Issues include cheating, ghosting friends, and two-faced friends.

2. Ask students to find their partner based on the title of their card. The scenario will be the same on both cards but with a different viewpoint on the best strategy to handle the situation.

3. Let students debate with one another, defending the viewpoint of their card.

4. Share what happened in a larger group during their discussion. Was there a clear right or wrong? Were both viewpoints right or wrong? How did it feel to argue the perspective they received? Was it hard to argue a perspective they didn't agree with?

5. What insights did they gain about their own morals or ethical code?

Idea #44: Give students space and time.

We need to provide space and time for students to learn more about themselves and have more opportunities for reflection and introspection. Below are four specific ways to make this happen:

#1: Feedback box. Direct students to write their names on a paper. Pass the paper around the class so each student can write the top trait they think of when reflecting on the person named on the sheet. This exercise will allow the students to see how others view them and provide them with more depth to their introspection journey.

#2: Journal entry. Ask the students to write a daily or weekly journal emphasizing their reflective thoughts. This will help them with their metacognition and their ability to articulate their thoughts.

#3: Artwork. Encourage them to develop a self-portrait or have them draw what they care about.

#4: Journalism. Assign them to cover and develop a story about something they distinctly care about. The students need to experience the sensation of creating an original product to gain a deeper connection to what matters to them.

Idea #45: Keep a CD (cognitive dissonance) weekly journal.

Cognitive dissonance is the discomfort created when two cognitions (ways of thinking) are incompatible with each other. Understanding the components of cognitive dissonance can help us gain a better understanding of the complexity of moral ambiguity. We all deal with cognitive dissonance issues that place stress on our understanding of right and wrong and ethical behavior. For example, who can relate to trying to lose a few pounds and finding yourself famished, tempted, and conflicted by the dessert on the counter right before you go to bed? It takes discipline and resistance from the incompatible thoughts of forgoing the sweet to lose weight versus indulging in the delicious snack in front of you.

So what does cognitive dissonance have to do with this chapter? Our goal in presenting an activity on cognitive dissonance is to help kids realize that acting on what they say is important is vital to their moral and ethical growth, but it isn't easy.

Here's what you can do to set up the cognitive dissonance activity modeled after an exercise found in the publication *Practical Psychology.* Help students develop a CD journal for one week. At the end of each day, the students could chart these two prompts:

1. What experiences in their day made them feel guilty?

2. In what ways did they rationalize any of their behavior?

After one week, engage the students in an open discussion by asking this question:

> *How did your week of charting your behaviors of guilt and rationalization teach you more deeply about the impact of cognitive dissonance on our ethical approach?*

This activity can get personal, so make sure your students are comfortable sharing. Also, we designed this activity for older classes, so we encourage you to modify it accordingly.

CHAPTER 10

INSPIRE CHANGEMAKERS

Equip students with constructive ways to take different pathways to action

We cannot always build a future for our youth, but we can always build our youth for the future.

— FRANKLIN D. ROOSEVELT

Essential Question: How can we empower students to use their agency to make a difference?

Objective: Help students develop skills so they can turn problems into possibilities.

THE PROBLEM: STUDENTS FEEL DISEMPOWERED TO TAKE ACTION

THE WORLD ISN'T fair, and for children, it doesn't take long to notice. Children are quick to recognize disparities from an early age and question the system as soon as it doesn't add up with their innocent outlook on what's right versus wrong. For instance, a kindergartner might wonder why another student gets cookies in their lunchbox while they're stuck eating the vegetables that were put in theirs. Answer that to an outraged five-year-old! The Christmas holiday has apparent flaws that youngsters are quick to notice. Why would "Santa" give more toys to kids who already have a lot of toys and not just give more toys to the kids who don't have as many? That doesn't add up, either.

It's hard to know how to respond to kids when they face an injustice, no matter how trivial. Kids are constantly exploring their worlds, and observing injustices troubles them. They notice when animals are hurt, litter is on the ground, people are mean, or when people are sleeping on the street. They start questioning at a young age. As adults, we usually have two ways to approach their questioning. We can tell them to accept the world as is, or we can empower them to act as a changemaker. When we focus on the latter, we can tap into the wonder of each child and help them use sense-making to discover why the world works that way or what causes those problems. From there, if they feel something is unjust or the world isn't working the way they feel it should, we can provide them with healthy outlets to take action.

When life feels unfair and doesn't match up with our vision of what it could be, it can sometimes be hard to cope. Children are often idealists with the energy and drive to make a change, and we should nurture that energy so it lasts within them for as long as possible. Perhaps it's because we, ourselves, weren't always given practical strategies to become active and involved, but as adults, we tend to grow tired and weary of the world's problems. Issues can seem so overwhelming that it becomes easiest to admit defeat and accept that it's just the way it is. We may even tell our children and our students the same. That doesn't have to be the reality, though. There's always something we can do to make a situation better, no matter how small. Change takes time, and small acts performed by many people add up, as we previously discussed in our chapter on collective leadership. We don't always need heroes or grand acts to create positive change. If everyone were to live their best lives, be kind, and do their work ethically, it would make for a much fairer and more desirable world.

It's the "doing something" that matters most, and we wonder if some of the polarization we see stems from a lack of agency to do good. It's easy to blame and complain if we don't like how things are, but the reality is this mindset often forms complacency and inaction. When we wait for others to solve the problems, it enables those who scream the loudest (often on polarizing ends of the spectrum) to have more power than they should, and it drives initiatives we don't necessarily agree with.

Being a good citizen shouldn't be that hard. Somehow, the idea of "doing good" has become an extra and something we've over-complicated. Being decent and caring about your community and the world should be the norm. It's not difficult to *do something*. At the most basic level, we can each do our best to act ethically, treat people with kindness, and hold ourselves accountable for our actions. These should be staples of how we lead our lives. Most of the injustices we see in the world may have a root in some larger systemic problem, but they trickle down, and we feel them in our daily occurrences. It's in *how* we live and work that we each can make our mark.

> **When we expose students to methodologies that allow for creative problem-solving and entrepreneurial thinking, we're helping them understand how to find the opportunity and resilience they need to push forward when challenges arise.**

As adults, what steps and strategies are we providing to our youth so they grow up to become adults who know how to handle a complicated world? Life may be full of problems, but it is also full of opportunities. Let's strive to help our students identify the possibility that lies within every problem and provide enough guidance on *how* they might take action so they understand what that can look like. When students find a problem they feel matters, something worth fighting for, they should understand how they might find constructive ways to do their part. We need to help young people identify where they can find their place and purpose in this world, and there are many ways to do that.

THE SOLUTION: INSPIRE CHANGEMAKERS

We describe a changemaker as someone who uses their agency to advance change for the good of all. Every young person should not only recognize they have the power to make a difference, but they also have the skills to act on their ideas. They should feel a sense of accountability about what they will contribute to the world. This is our last skillbuilder for a reason. Building on the previous nine chapters, it's now time to take that constructive dialogue to the next level and equip our students with processes that facilitate action.

To us, changemaking is about applying entrepreneurial thinking to the causes we care about. Entrepreneurial thinking is similar to creative problem-solving. It's a process through which we harness the knowledge, wisdom, resources, and skills at their disposal to do something about challenges we face (e.g., bullying, drugs, or discrimination, to name a few). There's often no "right" way to solve these challenges, and this might be one reason we often don't practice entrepreneurial thinking in our schools. Our students need it, however, as "getting their hands dirty" offers the best playing field for them to exercise the critical skills they can gain from this sort of problem-solving. In engaging with these challenges, students learn empathy, teamwork, transformational leadership, and project management.

Changemaking has proven to lend itself to our personal well-being, as we find joy and purpose in our ability to work on what matters to us. It not only makes for a better society, but it can also open the doors to new opportunities and new types of work. That's why it's important that students get a chance to practice designing and implementing ideas they believe will make a difference.

Processes like human-centered design or agile methodology provide opportunities for us to engage students in entrepreneurial thinking. It's through these processes that students connect their strengths (e.g., the arts, sports, technology, engaging with others) to the issues they care about (e.g., social justice, climate action, poverty). Maker spaces, genius hours, service learning, and volunteering provide spaces for us to support students' passion projects or to help them gain new skills as they tackle the problems that interest them. What's critical with changemaking is that we provide the time and space for students to use their own agency to work toward a solution they've created.

When we expose students to methodologies that allow for creative problem-solving and entrepreneurial thinking, we're helping them understand how to find the opportunity and resilience they need to push forward when challenges arise. It's through these projects (or inventions, initiatives, experiments, or whatever they choose to design) that students realize how to harness their power to do something impactful. While changemaking might bring joy, it's not necessarily easy. As we coach students to work toward the changes they seek to create, we help to manage expectations so they don't get disappointed when their efforts feel futile. It's vital that we discuss ideas like impact so they think critically about how they tackle problems and how to pivot when things don't go as planned. Through changemaking, they learn how to make their ideas grow, how to evolve them, and when to let them go.

We don't need everyone to care about or attempt to solve every problem. We don't need to be experts in everything. But we need to trust that those closest to the problem are usually closest to the solution. Equipping every student to act as a changemaker would ensure that every student, regardless of their role in society, had the know-how to make a difference. We all have our roles to play, and changemaking can build that trust we need in one another so we realize that we are each out there doing our best, which is critical to a functioning society and a robust democracy.

Your student or child should be ready to actively take part as a productive member of the society in which you live. We need consensus-building, we need constructive dialogue, and we desperately need people to get involved and take action. It's about working together as a democracy to protect our livelihoods, our world, and humanity. Even if these efforts fail, we must at least try. Democracy is precious. If we, the people, are not actively involved, then are we truly living in a democracy? And if we aren't equipping students with the tools to do something, to take action, are we not just laying the groundwork for a new set of disgruntled adults who are angry because of their powerlessness or complacent because the problems have become so overwhelming that they don't know what to do? Let's make sure we're giving our youngsters the tools and the mindsets to shape the world they will soon inherit.

CIVICS CONNECTION: EQUIP STUDENTS FOR CIVIC ENGAGEMENT

Inaction can spark feelings of hopelessness and powerlessness, which can lead to intense feelings of frustration and even anger. When people don't learn how to manage these emotions and find constructive outlets to do something with the injustices that ignite them, bad things can happen, and hatred can grow. People might turn to fruitless efforts like social media wars, or they may pick unnecessary fights with others to feel heard.

We think this tenth skillbuilder is the culminating skill to develop. Here's why: We tell students their voices matter, but do they? In the civics classroom, it can cause you to question just how much truth there might be to that statement. In the education space, there's a lot of empty talk on "voice and choice," the opportunity to choose to learn the way we learn best and to direct some aspects of our learning concretely and productively. But what does that look like in reality?

As adults, how much voice and choice do we have in shaping our world? We say this because our students will often point out just how senseless it all seems. As we discuss the multitude of issues that plague us—past, present, and future—and the role of the government, some students notice just how slow progress comes. These students question why we aren't more advanced as a society, why certain problems get ignored, or why people aren't working to fix parts of our system that aren't working. Some students want to know what they can do to change things and how they can make a difference. What are the pathways to action?

On the other side of the pendulum are the students who are already questioning why they should bother. They don't even want the responsibility of voice and choice, perhaps because we have conditioned them to live without it. They may have already settled into the mindset that the world will never change, so it's not their problem. Others genuinely believe the world is so wonderful that there's no need to change anything. They may be unaware of many realities in the world and can sometimes get mad at the students who want to take action.

We're stuck in this interesting situation where students largely fall into two camps. The first camp is excited and ready to go but doesn't have the tools or know-how to act. The second camp needs to be convinced they have a responsibility to be engaged members of society. Admittedly, given that we only have students for four to nine months of the academic year, it's not enough time to instill the mindset or the skillset needed to ensure all students are actively engaged citizens. But we must strive to make our time with them as productive and impactful as possible.

This shows that changemaking matters. It's critical that we help students from all spectrums appreciate that democracy is what gives them a voice in the first place and that we must protect it. For democracy to work, students need the opportunity to put their agency to good use. We don't need everyone to care about the same things; society needs each person to find their niche and where they can make the most impact. One person's desire for sustainable packaging will not match another's quest for educational reform. And that's okay. It's actually preferable.

We want to equip students to find opportunities in the problems they come across. As we alluded to earlier, those closest to the problem are often closest to the solution. Imagine if we equipped every child with a mindset and the skills to do something about the problems they will inevitably come across in their lives. They could improve society and create jobs, and we would help more young people find their purpose.

Unfortunately, we often lack adequate resources to equip students to be civically engaged. To our dismay, the curriculum rarely offers much insight or emphasizes the gravity of this work. Most schools don't have courses on changemaking, agility, or design thinking that equip students with skills like empathy and creative problem-solving. So, the civics classroom ends up serving as a critical space for guidance on how to solve problems, which is challenging when we have little support. In many civics texts, the dialogue about getting involved is outdated. It seems like an end-all on how to be civic-minded and engaged, and the list often looks like this:

1. Vote

2. Protest

3. Sign a petition

4. Write to an official

5. Run for office

6. Donate

7. Join an organization

That's a limiting view of how you can shape your world, and it's no wonder most people don't get involved. It feels completely disjointed to modern, daily life, which is a ridiculous precedent to set for students who we need to be political. Policies shape every aspect of our lives, and we can do more to be civically engaged in caring for our communities and shaping our world. Given how narrow this list is, it's understandable that so many individuals feel powerless or don't correlate policy to the world around them. Most of these initiatives do nothing to help validate people's efforts, nor help them feel like they're taking action. In fact, they can sometimes have the opposite effect and fuel a sense of powerlessness. As problems persist, voting, petitioning, protesting, and reaching out to legislators can sometimes make you feel even smaller and more worthless as years pass and nothing changes.

Since hardly anyone lives in a direct democracy where citizens vote specifically and directly on policies and laws, those in representative democracies might need to get even more creative with how we get things done. We can do many things—in fact, we *have* to do them—to ensure our government works on our behalf. If we don't, it becomes that much harder for individual citizens, businesses, and organizations to compensate by addressing the inadequacies that come with poor policies. So, what does it look like to be civically engaged? What should the list in the civics text look like so students understand how to be good and active citizens?

To us, it's simple. If we want to direct students on how to be civically engaged, to inspire changemakers, the list should look more like this:

1. *Make yourself accountable.* Students must recognize that to protect democracy, we each should be our best selves in our actions and words. Feeling a sense of responsibility for the demands of our delicate world is a key piece of starting our changemaker journey. This doesn't need to be complicated. As we have mentioned, doing good should be the norm; being a good citizen is as simple as staying informed and contributing to society by being a decent person and doing decent work. As citizens, we have a responsibility to give back to society and not just take. We could build up our trust again in society if everyone did their part.

2. *Keep learning.* Are we as informed as we think we are? Do we make good decisions? Are we open? Thinking about impact means being able to evaluate the effect an initiative, activity, project, or policy will have on people and communities because of an action or inaction. When students can think in terms of impact, they can evaluate which policies are effective or what's a good use of their time as they make efforts to shape their world.

3. *Contribute toward good policy.* Recognizing systems-level change is all about good leader-ship and policy. The bare minimum we can do to work toward this is to stay up-to-date on issues, be

thoughtful about the leaders we elect, vote, petition, and write letters. We may not feel our impact, but these efforts, though more traditional, do matter. It's important we make it clear to our students that this list is not finite and that when we really care about something, we might achieve our goals in many ways, including the basics (e.g., voting at all levels).

4. *Find meaning in your work and daily life.*
Find your purpose with how you choose to spend your days. This is where changemaking comes into play. How we lead our lives determines the type of difference we make. Where will you make your mark, not just for yourself, but for your family, your community, or the world? We each have something of value to offer. At the most basic level, you can do every job ethically. This means whatever you do, do it right. Don't take shortcuts. Treat people well. Don't engage in work that is harmful. We can create, build, invent, and improve systems from within (e.g., intrapreneurship). If students focus on the types of problems they want to solve, it can guide them on their personal and career journeys as they explore different paths that make things better. Are we challenging them to find this purpose?

5. *Remember impact over ego.* This is about "we before me." We need to work together to make significant improvements (think of the waste-reduction example) and remember the power of collective leadership. The bigger the problem, the less likely we are to feel our impact. That doesn't mean we give up. We tend to give up when we don't receive recognition or

rewards for our efforts. When you keep the idea or goal in mind, it's easier to push forward. We go further together, which is why we must join forces and feel united as citizens.

6. *Take changemaking to new levels.* Challenge students to create the change they want to see. Share ideas, start new programs, invent, build, up-cycle, write, start a social business, be an activist, research, and question norms. Young people can do so many activities to be good citizens who make a difference. Are we empowering them to take bold steps?

Remember that sometimes, all it takes is one voice to make a change. If not you, then who?

A few years ago in Illinois, a young woman took democracy into her own hands. Lisa Creason was nineteen years old when she made a horrible and desperate decision to find money to help raise her small child by robbing a local restaurant. Her arrest and subsequent trial verdict put her in prison for some time and made it so she couldn't get certain jobs upon her release from prison. She tried to turn her life around upon being released but realized she wasn't eligible to receive a nursing license in Illinois per state law because of her felony charge. This heart-wrenching reality became a moment of truth for Lisa. Instead of giving up on her dream of becoming a nurse, she became an activist.

For well over a year, she lobbied members of the Illinois State General Assembly in Springfield. She worked relentlessly to get lawmakers to rethink a law put on the books in 2011 that added attempted robbery as one of the felonies that would deny someone work in certain licensed occupations, including nursing. Her focus and diligence ultimately paid off as she convinced lawmakers to change the law and then influenced the governor of Illinois to sign this revised law in 2016. Lisa Creason went from down and out in prison to an activist lobbying to change laws.

This great story of living in a democracy should inspire all of us to understand that we can make a difference, even though it might be a bit of a daunting story. Do you have to lobby Congress to make a difference? No. Policy might be one way to create the greatest impact, but it's not the only path we have to be engaged and active citizens. Most people don't have the access or opportunities to directly push lawmakers, whether at the local, state, or federal level, to establish legislation to directly benefit the cause these people are promoting. More realistically, students need to understand that all our actions, both great and small, add up and can truly make a difference in driving change.

MAKE THIS SKILL A REALITY

Eight billion people live on the planet. With limited resources and a dramatically changing world, we need a mindset shift now more than ever. Every individual should understand they have a purpose and their actions matter. Educators can help to ensure that the next generation has the opportunity to uncover who they are and what they offer. Humanity may just depend on it.

We could have easily made this section another book. In fact, in my (Michelle) book, *The Startup Teacher Playbook*, my coauthor and I lay the groundwork for making ideas come to life through a holistic approach that combines transformational leadership, project management, agility, and well-being. There are countless ways to be a needle mover. Doing good, caring about your community, and helping to shape the world can come in so many sizes and packages that it feels almost overwhelming when we think about starting points. So before we get into the activities, let's look at just how easy it can be to bring this concept of being a good citizen into all we do as teachers.

We need to help make the connection for students that they can do anything for the better. Even for those children who only want to make a lot of money, they can check the world of ESG funds (environmental, social, and governance), learn about green finance, or look at data that shows the value (profits!) of investing in women. For the students interested in science, how can they make their invention to help people or to improve processes and systems (for example, how might we produce more sustainable building materials or methodologies that improve irrigation)? For our athletes, how can we use sports to contribute to an important cause? We can always use our talents, interests, strengths, and skills for good. Maybe you bring joy, spark a connection, or solve a problem that impacts many. It's our job as educators to show what being a good citizen looks like and how to use our uniqueness to contribute.

How can we create outlets for students to find their purpose and place? How can we encourage all students to be good citizens? Let's explore these questions in five categories.

1. **Mindset:** How can we help students think differently about "doing good" and their role as citizens?
   Doing good isn't just going to the soup kitchen. It's about living our ideals every day in what we do and how we interact with others. It's about holding ourselves accountable and taking responsibility for our actions and how they might impact others.

2. **Content:** How do we add a narrative to our curriculum that emphasizes relevant, real-world challenges that students might engage in?

   All content can apply to good. It's all about the story we tell with how to apply the content. Use each of these examples to teach good citizenship in action:

- ► *English:* Dissect character and social movements. Let students use literature to see that these dilemmas have all happened before. Let them reflect on how attitudes and events have impacted history.

- ► *Math:* Statistics, exponential growth, and measuring impact. Numbers are what give us insights. If you don't understand what numbers tell us, you remain ignorant of their relevance and gravity.

- ► *Finance:* Green finance, investing in women, and social business. Can we help prove that the false dichotomy that we must choose between money or the environment no longer exists?

- ► *Science:* What can we invent to solve problems? New materials, new processes, and new cures. What advancements does the world need?

3. **Pedagogy:** Are we facilitating learning experiences that encourage students to build their changemaker skills?

Service learning, project-based learning, design thinking, changemaking, community service, activism, storytelling, STEM, and art are all mediums through which we can teach students how to do good. How are you weaving in opportunities for students to build skills and take action with the content you deliver? How are you incorporating the purpose and relevance to the content they learn? This will set the foundation for how they push ideas forward as adults.

4. **Tech Integration:** Are we tapping into our students' technology skills so they understand how to use those skills for good?

How can we harness the power of technology for good? How do we model and act as good citizens virtually?

5. **Assessments:** Are we assessing in a way that promotes skillbuilding and encourages students to take healthy risks?

Have students design and create something that matters, even if it's a mock-up. Create an opportunity: design a project, program, organization, or company that does good. Write, make art, produce a film, or start a campaign.

STRATEGIES YOU CAN IMPLEMENT RIGHT AWAY

Idea #46: Showcase how to use tech for good.

It seems like a trend exists among people to view technology with a negative lens. In this book, we have mentioned many of the perils and challenges that technology can bring to our students. But of course, it's not that simple. While we need to teach the realities of technology, part of those realities is an infinite potential for good. As teachers, let's not lose sight of that fact.

Idea #47: Encourage service learning.

Pick any issue and become an activist. Here's an example of what a service-learning project might look like. (I, Brian, have modified this model from a former colleague of mine in my civics classes for the last several years.)

Service-learning project: instructions for students

Service learning is the integration of meaningful community service with instruction and reflection to enrich the learning experience, teach civic responsibility, and strengthen communities.

You will hand in a typed plan of action. This plan of action includes a thorough plan of all the steps you would take to make this plan a reality. Explain and cite (as applicable) all the following parts:

- ► What is the problem, and why do you care?
- ► Who did you talk to? Why?
- ► Who are you writing to? Why?
- ► What are your add-ons? Why will this help your cause?

You will write a simulated formal letter to a person, group, or organization. In the letter, you will discuss a concern you have and what you think they should fix or make better to help improve the community impacted by that concern. Your letter should include a suggestion (or more than one) with specific details about what you think they should do to help inform and activate interest to help solve the issue, problem, or concern. Make certain to mention your add-on within your letter.

You will create an add-on. This add-on helps convince people to support the goal mentioned in your letter. Below is a list of options, but these are just a few suggestions.

- ► Write a newspaper editorial.
- ► Create a mock web social media page.

- ▶ Create public-service announcements or advertising of some sort (audio, video, or pamphlet).
- ▶ Plan and host an event (informational, advocacy, fundraising)—Your plan would include the details of what you would do for the event to make it a reality.
- ▶ Create a club, group, or organization. Explain what that group does and how you will get members.

Finally, you will also give an oral report on an assigned day. Your report will discuss:

- ▶ What did you decide to do?
- ▶ What research did you do?
- ▶ Why did you choose to suggest that add-on?
- ▶ What did you learn along the way?
- ▶ If you had carried it out, what successes and failures do you think you would have? How would you improve the project if you had to do it all over again?

Idea #48: Play the *Apprentice Game* about entrepreneurial thinking, mindset, and changemaking.

To encourage students to think as changemakers, one fun role-playing game is the Apprentice Game. Group students in fours or fives and have them come up with a way to solve a problem. Each group must deal with the same issue but needs to have its own rules of engagement to solve the issue productively. You can be the "boss" at the end to decide which team has produced the best idea.

Here's one quick example of an option you could pose to your class:

iPads in the Classroom: Whereas it is a wonderful tool in a classroom for all students to have a device, it can come with distractions and things that limit learning.

In your group, develop a five-step plan that works to magnify the learning enhancements of this technology while minimizing the distracting obstacles. Go!

Idea #49: Deploy modern assessments.

Let's challenge ourselves as teachers to vary our assessments. Moving away at times from traditional types of student assessment (whether formative or summative) can truly benefit students as we prepare them for the realities of living in this twenty-first century. Try new methods of assessments like problem-based learning modules, simulations, or anything that is hands-on.

Idea #50: Play *Challenge Question Mad Libs* to nurture interests and promote risk-taking.

Let students explore what interests them. Most changemakers succeeded because they had someone who noticed that they cared about something and supported that curiosity. We need to encourage learning and growth by taking chances, even failing at times, to grow as changemakers.

One way to allow this exploration is through the Challenge Question Mad Libs activity (taken from *The Startup Teacher Playbook*). See Image 10.1.

WRITE YOUR CHALLENGE QUESTION
How might I/We ACTION + USER + IMPACT ?

CHALLENGE QUESTION

Image 10.1

Have students brainstorm the following:

Impact

- What bothers you?
- What do you care about?
- What are others talking or complaining about?

When finished, have students circle the response that resonates the most with them.

Action

- What interests you?
- List some of your strengths.

When finished, have students circle the response they feel the most strongly about.

Users

- Who (your friends, your school, your community) or what (plants, animals, etc.) would your actions impact?

When finished, pick the one you feel would be the most likely to be impacted.

Now synthesize and put your challenge question together using Image 10.1 as a guide. You may not solve it immediately, but it's a challenge to pose to yourself so when you see the opportunity to put your strengths and interests together, you can act.

BUILD THE SKILLS TO BECOME CONNECTED, INFORMED, AND ENGAGED CITIZENS

S OCIAL STUDIES COURSES—civics, history, and others—were never meant to be taught only as facts and figures. These courses help us understand the world we live in, observe how societies function, identify patterns in history, explore how resources and geography impact how we live and work, and understand how systems and policies shape our practices and worldviews. But that's not necessarily what's happening.

Often, we've gone down the wrong path. There's not anyone to blame. Like the polarization we've spoken about throughout the book, we need to recognize that the milk has been spilled and now we need to clean it up. We speak from experience when we say it's not always easy to get back on track. We understand the struggle that comes from teaching a subject dictated by poorly constructed standardized tests (that largely assess for memorization rather than understanding), which exacerbate the situation. Many social studies classrooms have become places where teachers force students to memorize dates and facts, items that are easily Googled. The social studies curriculum, and we assume it's the same for many other subjects, should provide a platform for us to ensure our students are prepared for the world they are about to inherit.

Let's strive to have realistic conversations about the current state of the world and what our future holds. The future is now. What we do today will impact tomorrow, and if you're paying attention, you'll quickly see that most predictions aren't very optimistic. It's important that we reflect on and refocus our efforts so we can make social studies and civics classes be what they're supposed to be: preparation for being an engaged citizen so we're equipped to brave whatever storms come our way. In doing so, people could better understand concepts like how the government works, government priorities (or what those priorities should be), if laws are being broken, and if a free and fair election is happening. Social studies and civics classes need to provide pathways for citizens to get involved in helping to combat ignorance, which can potentially lend itself to manipulation.

Social studies classes are meant to act as our practice field. They are our space to learn how to have constructive dialogues on complicated issues and to build consensus around how we might tackle the challenges we face. They should not be designed to be restrictive of viewpoints and opinions. If we take someone's experience out of the narrative, then we are making ourselves more vulnerable to losing our freedoms. We should be able to be exposed to everything and entertain all thoughts in order to truly live in a democratic society. General Mark Milley, chair of the US Joint Chiefs of Staff, was recently questioned about the growing controversy of teaching critical race theory in American schools. He poignantly responded to fear-driven concerns by stating, "I've read Mao Zedong. I've read Karl Marx. I've read Lenin. That doesn't make me a communist." We include this quote because it is at the essence of what we must advocate as civics teachers: don't run from the views and experiences of others: learn from them. As teachers and classroom leaders, be brave enough to have these tough talks and get uncomfortable. Your silence is more dangerous than not discussing these issues at all!

Without pursuing holistic knowledge, our students can become vulnerable to extreme beliefs and institutions. The path to radical views is not that difficult of a path to find yourself on. In fact, that path may be one we find easy to travel on. It may seem comfortable and even useful, depending on our needs and visions. But these types of paths move us further apart from the road that we all need to be on to achieve a functional existence. We all must be able to read the road signs warning us of the perils this path can throw at us, or we will continue on the paths that divide us. The path to political mayhem, revolutions, and war is a slow burn, and people often don't even realize it. It's like the adage about the frog being boiled in hot water. If the temperature rises slowly over time, the frog isn't even aware of his fate. It is his complacency that facilitates this slow boil.

We all know that history is constantly vulnerable to repeating itself. Polarization is a path to destruction, and the ingredients are often the same. Look, for instance, at the constant cycle of history that clearly shows how situations like the rise of fascism emerge. Authoritarianism, autocracy, and absolutism have proven time and again to be byproducts of an uninformed population. Uninformed people are vulnerable to dangerous misinformation.

In this book, we have tried hard to hit home the concerning reality that we are losing the bar on truth. And once we don't know who to believe anymore, we find ourselves in a terrible "rabbit hole." Frankly, we don't have decades more to be drifting down this rabbit hole, remaining unaware of reality. Add it up: population growth plus minimal resources plus climate issues equals: We have to change our ways if we want to give humanity a chance. We're not trying to be prophets of doom, but within the next century, there is a real risk of societal collapses around the globe. We must do what we can to encourage people—our students, specifically—to do something. Students need to be knowledgeable and motivated.

As US founding father John Adams once stated, "Liberty cannot be preserved without general knowledge among the people, who have a right … and a desire to know." And as a warning shot to inspire us to continue to do the work to prevent polarization, he also said, "Remember, democracy never lasts long. It soon wastes, exhausts, and murders itself. There never was a democracy yet that did not commit suicide."

This quote made us reflect on January 6, 2021. What happened at the United States Capitol on that fateful day is the consummate example of why we have felt impassioned to write this book. As Americans, seeing this important icon under assault when we turned on the news was shocking. Despite this shock, it also was an event that was all too predictable. One of the dark-humored memes that came out that day read:

"Well, that escalated slowly over four years."

This meme applies to people who have been paying attention, who have learned to study patterns of history, and who have collected thoughts on absorbing information, understanding how governments work and how fragile they can be, especially when manipulated by lies and demagoguery. But our view, sadly, is that the number of citizens who have had access to civic education that instills these skills is becoming fewer and fewer, both in the United States and around the globe. You may feel the same way, which may be why you picked up our book and have made it this far in reading it.

But so many other people truly could not wrap their minds around the idea that a group of Americans who love their country could bring violence to the nation's capital. The reason for their genuine shock must connect to their vision of the world, particularly a worldview impacted by their media influences. So many of us know this to be true. And so many of us want to do the right thing, but we now feel that we are "damned if we do and damned if we don't" regarding trying to be vocal to make a difference. We know it is a psychological nightmare out there in the world of social media and beyond. You feel compelled to make a point about something you believe passionately in, only to have it attacked and twisted into a cyberspace shouting match.

But let's not end on such an ominous note. Let's hope that we can play a role in bringing people to greater awareness and engagement. When done right, democracy has always proven in history to be the best form of government to allow people to maintain their natural rights. As the colorful Winston Churchill once put it, "Democracy is the worst form of government, except for all the others."

We hope you have become more introspective throughout this read. We encourage you to implement our skillbuilders into your classroom, home, or community as you see fit. Despite the psychological nightmare we can easily find ourselves in on Twitter or Facebook or at the holiday dinner table, we must have the courage to combat this debilitating polarization. It's our responsibility as educators to combat this. We want what's best for our students, and implementing the skills we have laid out in this book will help pave their future. We need them to have the skills to navigate the path forward, to solve the problems we've created, and to lead a good life. If you help students build these skills, we truly believe that students will have the mindset to learn about civics and to begin truly understanding their government. It will enable civics not to be abstract and students to understand they can engage in it and do something about *now*—for their future.

Let's keep aspiring to do it right. Let's keep remembering that we, as educators, are on the front lines in the battle to keep the future full of informed and engaged citizens actively involved in ensuring their governments work for them. We want them to feel empowered and encouraged to be political. Being political should be virtuous. Being in politics should be a profession that attracts ethical and moral people. It is our challenge and duty to promote this notion to our students.

Thank you for giving us your time and attention as we all move forward together as advocates for improving this world through education. Here's to preventing polarization by strengthening civic-mindedness and promoting more consensus in society.

APPENDIX

A S WE STATED in the Introduction, we want to provide you with some space here at the end of the book to consider how these skills may fit into your class environment.

Design time: What would work best in your classroom?

As much as we love sharing skillbuilders, we realize you have your own ideas in mind. As such, we want to support you as the creator you are and leave you with a space to design your own skillbuilder, activity, or project. Taken from *The Startup Teacher Playbook*, we present you with the Educator Canvas. This tool provides a space for you to create a blueprint of how you might implement your own idea.

Basically, the Educator Canvas is a series of guided questions to help you create a plan of action. We've found it's been incredibly useful in helping teachers implement their great ideas. If you've already got an idea of something you would like to try, see the images in this Appendix (or print them for free at theeducatorslab.com). If you need more time to figure out your next steps, here are suggestions to get you going.

The first step in the Educator Canvas is to ask yourself a challenge question. For instance, you might be wondering:

- What opportunities do I have to incorporate these skills into my instruction to promote consensus-building and civic-mindedness?

- How might I create spaces or opportunities for students to engage in difficult conversations so they become better at engaging in difficult dialogues?

- What activities can work in my classroom to help students build more self-awareness about how they interact with issues?

- How might I let students discuss or explore their frustrations in a constructive way?

- How can I get buy-in from staff or parents to engage in these dialogues so I can reduce pushback?

- How might I encourage students to do something about their frustrations so they understand the pathways to action at their disposal?

- How might I embed time in our schedule or instruction devoted to them taking action so students are equipped and supported to act?

Whatever your questions, we invite you to take time to reflect on your challenge so you uncover opportunities to try something new. Just like in the Mad Lib activity we presented earlier, what piece of the puzzle do you want to work on?

USER

Who are you designing for; who's the primary beneficiary of your work? Could be:

- other teachers
- your students
- parents/guardians
- school community

You can work at any level you want.

How might I/We (ACTION) + (USER) + (IMPACT)?

ACTION

A verb (phrase) describing how you will work on your problem.

IMPACT

The goal of your action.

Having a measurable outcome will help you assess whether or not your approach to the problem had the desired impact.

Image A.1: How to Write a Challenge Question

If you know you'd like to do something but you're not quite sure what to choose, here's a bit of brainstorming support. In the Educator Canvas, you'll see space to write a solution. This space is not meant for you to come up with the silver bullet that will end all problems (if only!). This space is for you to write down an idea you might like to *try*. That said, there are often many things we could do to address our challenges. Here's a quick exercise to help you think through your ideas. Afterward, we suggest you try out the idea you think will have the greatest impact but is also the easiest to implement (in other words, the most needed and the most practical).

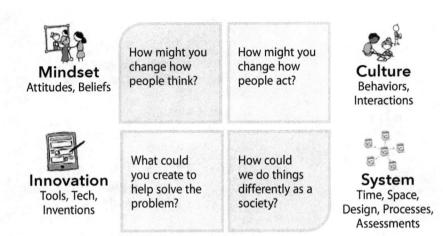

Image A.2: Mindset, Culture, Innovation, and System

Once you have an idea of the problem you are trying to solve (e.g., your challenge question) and what you might like to try (e.g., your solution), The Educator Canvas can take it from there. Fill in the boxes to create your own project or initiative. And remember, there's no such thing as failure. Anything you try will get you one step closer to equipping your students with the skills they need to build consensus and prevent polarization!

Educator CANVAS

PROBLEM Write your problem as a single statement or question.

Project Name

Short-Term Goals
- What would success look like?
- How might you measure your goals?
- How is your project creating value for others?

Inspiration
- What evidence can you find to validate that this idea could work?
- What tools or strategies could you use or adopt to help you implement?

Long-Term Vision
- Is this a one-off project or a piece of a bigger picture?
- How do short-term goals fit into a longer-term vision?

User Input
- How will you get buy-in from your user?
- How do you plan to get feedback on your solution from your user?

IMPACT

INSIGHTS

Created by

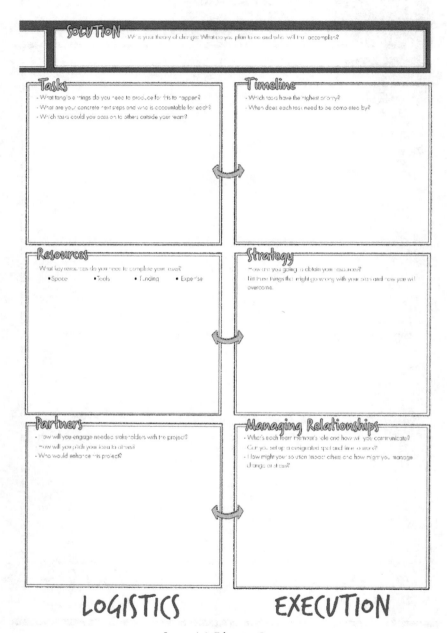

Image A.3: Educator Canvas

SNEAK PEEK

THE PROBLEM: TEACHERS ASSUME A CORRECT ANSWER MEANS THE STUDENT "GOT IT"

MANY TEACHERS USE questions to check for student understanding of concepts and learning, then use correct responses as evidence that the students "got it." The trouble with using answers to determine proficiency is that answers are not transferable. Logical thinking and reasoning are transferable. When we expect that a right answer today is an indication of right answers for life, we find ourselves baffled when students are not able to repeat their thinking the very next day.

Hearing a right answer from a student frequently causes teachers to assume that students used a sound thinking process to reach that answer. But they rarely validate that assumption. If we don't ask students to *justify* their answers, it's like watching a music video on mute. We ignore the best part: the lullaby of logical reasoning. Sometimes students guess. Sometimes they memorize answers. Sometimes they are led to the right response through a line of well-intended spoon-feeding.

Our reaction to incorrect answers is equally important. Answer-seeking teachers might hear a wrong answer and say, "That's not exactly what I was looking for …" or "Hmm … who can help Jeremiah with this question?" This is a missed opportunity to reveal, address, and redirect misconceptions before students develop them into truths.

This action also communicates to the student that his learning is not the priority but announcing the right answer is the priority. If another student knows the right answer, it gives the teacher a sense that the students learned and that it is okay to move on with the lesson. The assumption is that the student who didn't know the answer will suddenly understand, simply by hearing the right answer from a peer. It is likely that this peer already knew the answer, though, so the result is that neither student experiences new learning.

Teachers foster fixed mindsets when they only welcome and celebrate right answers. The solution is simple: Answer-seeking perspective needs a change of tune.

THE HACK: HEAR THE MUSIC

We can almost hear a choir joining in a collective "ahhhh" when a student declares an answer and it is right.

Alternately, virtual alarms sound off in an experienced teacher's head when a string of erroneous answers pour out of a child's mouth. But we need to listen to what lies beyond the answers. Mute the choir or alarms until you hear the music behind how the student reached those answers. Take the additional step and ask the student to expose his thought process. This allows you to make sure he has a solid path of logic that he can replicate in different settings. It also provides students with the opportunity to be metacognitive about their learning. How did I get to this answer? Does my thinking make sense? Are there any exceptions to my assumptions? Am I certain, or do I still have some wonderings?

To get inside a student's head, use justification questions. Use them when the student's answer is correct ... *and* when the answer is clearly not correct. Maintain a poker face when requesting justification, or students will use social cues to influence how they articulate their thinking. Test this theory by asking a question typically reserved for wrong answers: "Are you sure?" When a student gives a right answer, watch how the student responds to "Are you sure?" It is a closed-ended, yes/no question that rarely solicits a yes/no answer. Even the youngest learners understand that this question is adult code for "Your answer is wrong."

Rather than triggering a mindframe of confusion and guessing, pose a question like, "How did you reach that response?" Their answers might surprise you. They may be over-generalizing old learning, or straight-out guessing.

For example, when learning about states of matter, Gabrielle shows her understanding from previous lessons by announcing, "Molecules in liquids move faster than molecules in solids." Ding! Correct! An answer-seeking teacher might be satisfied with the simple contrast regarding the speed of molecules. However, an expert teacher like science teacher Amy Miles is interested in how a student processes that information.

Consider what Gabrielle's response reveals when Mrs. Miles poses a follow-up question to Gabrielle's correct answer:

> Gabrielle: *Molecules in liquids move faster than molecules in solids.*
>
> Mrs. Miles: *What is an example?*
>
> Gabrielle: *Humans are solids. If I drink a lot of liquid, I will be able to run faster.*

At this point, teachers would notice that the student's response is way off-key. The alarms are screaming in our heads. It's tempting to interject with reteaching the idea of how the distance between molecules determines the state of matter and how it doesn't have anything to do with the physical movement of the human body. Instead of reteaching, though, ask the student to think about her thinking. Pose a question that uncovers the logic—or illogic, as the case may be. You'll uncover which part of the lesson the student truly understands and where she's getting confused. Gabrielle revealed where her understanding broke down when attempting to relate physical movement to the state of matter. A skilled educator continues with questions that push Gabrielle's assumptions and listens for the music of her logic.

Gabrielle: *That's because the molecules in the liquid will be moving faster than the rest of my body. Which will make me run faster. That's why my coach tells us to hydrate before track meets. It all makes sense now.*

Mrs. Miles: *You said humans are solid and the water you drink is liquid. Explain your thinking of how running faster connects to the movement of the molecules.*

Gabrielle: *If the molecules in the water mix with the molecules in my body, the slower molecules in my legs will speed up.*

Mrs. Miles: *So they mix together?*

Gabrielle: *Yes.*

Mrs. Miles: *What happens when they're mixed to help your legs speed up?*

Gabrielle: *Hmm, let me think about that. Maybe I'm not right.*

Mrs. Miles: *(pause) What scientific information makes you second-guess your thinking?*

Gabrielle: *If the molecules in my body started moving faster, then my body would turn to liquid, not run faster.*

Mrs. Miles: *What can you conclude from that?*

Gabrielle: *I was thinking that faster molecules would just move faster in every way. But that doesn't really make sense. Now I think that ...*

In this exchange, Mrs. Miles heard an alarm. She could see that Gabrielle was oversimplifying the information. She knew yesterday's lesson established a basic knowledge of solids, liquids, and gases, and that Gabrielle was using that knowledge incorrectly. Instead of indicating that Gabrielle's thinking was off, Mrs. Miles used prompts to help the student navigate through the information that was already in her head. The reasoning was in there, but she had not thought it through all the way.

Once you train yourself to listen for right thinking, you might find yourself saying, "That's music to my ears" in response to student reasoning. You will certainly be helping students to refine and utilize their thinking so it will reach further than giving one right answer.

THE HACK IN ACTION

Saranac Elementary School is dear to my heart; it has been my professional home for thirteen years as the principal and now curriculum director. One of the kindergarten teachers there, Barbara Cizauskas, is able to get five-year-olds to think hard and communicate clearly about their learning. Sometimes I have to remind myself that it is the first year of formal education for many of these young scholars because Mrs. Cizauskas makes their learning look so easy. How does she do it? She listens for the music.

A great example of this is how she used questions to listen to correct thinking—not just right answers—during math time. Mrs. Cizauskas was teaching students about the measurable attributes of shapes. This includes length, width, height, weight, and capacity. In a one-on-one exchange with a student, she began exploring ways to measure a tissue box—or as her mathematicians call it, a rectangular prism.

In the question-response process, she heard both music and alarms but figured out when to question and when to probe.

Moving students from surface understanding to deep understanding is music to our ears. To help us turn that music up, we sometimes have to tune in to thinking and focus less on the answer. Observe how you react to student answers. Remember, the response does not tell you how a student solved a problem or analyzed to reach that solution. Use probing questions to reveal how a student is processing content, and you'll start to hear the music. Stay away from leading questions that allow students to follow your thinking progression instead of developing their own.

The ultimate goal of learning is to maintain knowledge so it can be applied in context and transferred to relevant circumstances. Leading students to the right answer just to celebrate the arrival skips the music altogether. Ask yourself why you are posing a question. Is it simply to find someone who can prove they already knew it? Are you looking for students who might be left behind in the learning? Or is your purpose to analyze what students understand or don't understand yet, and why?

Do you hear music or alarms? Listen closely. Is it coming from right answers ... or right thinking?

ABOUT THE AUTHORS

Michelle Blanchet is an educator striving to improve how we treat, train, and value our teachers. After ten years of experience working with young people, she founded the Educators' Lab, which supports teacher-driven solutions to educational challenges.

Michelle earned a master's in international relations from Instituto de Empresa in Madrid. She has taught social studies in Switzerland and the US and has presented at many events, including SXSWedu and TEDxLausanne. Michelle is a part of the Global Shaper Community of the World Economic Forum. She has worked with organizations like PBS Education, the Center for Transformative Teaching and Learning, Ashoka, and the Center for Curriculum Redesign. She is the coauthor of *The Startup Teacher Playbook: How to Personalize Professional Learning for You and Your Students.*

Brian Deters has been in education for over twenty-seven years, teaching social studies and coaching varsity soccer in the United States and Switzerland. He continues to be an educator working to motivate his students to be more aware, more passionate, and more motivated to make a difference. Brian is also a co-host of the *4 A Better Tomorrow* podcast, a series that connects his teaching knowledge and experiences with his political ones, most notably his run in the 2018 election as a US Congressional primary candidate from the 18th District of Illinois.

Brian holds a bachelor's degree in secondary education from the University of Illinois in Urbana-Champaign and a master's degree in educational administration from Illinois State University, where he also served as an adjunct professor working in the field with student teachers in 2018 and 2019. He currently teaches sociology and civics at Morton High School in Morton, Illinois.

ACKNOWLEDGMENTS

W E'D LIKE TO thank a few people who have helped to make this book a reality. To a few editing eyes—Don Sturm, Ryan Lindley, Steve Blanchet, and Cathy Travis—we truly appreciate your willingness to read through our rough drafts and provide constructive support and critique throughout.

To our former and current social studies colleagues, thanks for your support, camaraderie, and inspirations. A special thanks needs to go out to someone who provided a tremendous amount of specific inspiration for many activities mentioned throughout this book: Thank you, Barb Katz.

To those who pushed our thinking and engaged us in thoughtful conversations. Thank you, Tim Logan and Bruno Taleb.

To the Times 10 Publications team for believing in our book and giving us the support we needed to make this a reality.

To our families for their love and patience and for giving us our motivation to pursue this project. We love you.

NOTES

Blanchet, Michelle, and Deters, Brian. *Civics Through Play*, civicsthroughplay.com.

Blanchet, Michelle, and Bakkegard, Darcy. *The Startup Teacher Playbook*. Times 10 Publications, 2021.

Blanchet, Michelle. *The Educators Lab*, theeducatorslab.com. Accessed 1 July 2022.

"Brainstorming Resources." *IDEO U*, ideou.com/pages/brainstorming-resources.

Itkowitz, Colby. "The law said an ex-felon couldn't be a nurse. So this single mom got the law changed." *Washington Post*, 26 Aug. 2016.

Leins, Casey. "Western States Lead Nation in Data Driven Policy." USNews.com, 7 Oct. 2019, usnews.com/news/best-states/articles/2019-10-07/western-states-lead-nation-in-data-driven-policy.

Muller, Brandon. "Download the Media Bias Chart." *Ad Fontes Media*, 16 Jan. 2022, https://adfontesmedia.com/static-mbc/.

Sargent, Mark K., et al. "Cognitive Dissonance (Definition + Examples)." *Practical Psychology*, 27 April 2022, http://www.practicalpie.com/cognitive-dissonance/. Accessed 1 July 2022.

"'Schools Are Killing Curiosity': Why We Need to Stop Telling Children to Shut up and Learn." *The Guardian*, Guardian News and Media, 28 Jan. 2020, https://www.theguardian.com/education/2020/jan/28/schools-killing-curiosity-learn.

MORE FROM
TIMES 10 PUBLICATIONS

Hacking School Discipline
9 Ways to Create a Culture of Empathy &
Responsibility Using Restorative Justice
Nathan Maynard and Brad Weinstein

Reviewers proclaim this Washington Post
Bestseller to be "maybe the most important
book a teacher can read, a must for all educators, fabulous, a game changer!" Teachers
and presenters Nathan Maynard and Brad
Weinstein demonstrate how to eliminate
punishment and build a culture of responsible students and independent learners in
a book that will become your new blueprint
for school discipline. Eighteen straight months at #1 on Amazon and
still going strong, *Hacking School Discipline* is disrupting education like
nothing we've seen in decades—maybe centuries.

Hacking Deficit Thinking
8 Reframes That Will Change the
Way You Think about Strength-Based
Practices and Equity in Schools
Byron McClure and Kelsie Reed

Transform learning by reframing your view
from what's wrong to what's strong.

"At risk." "Low." "Title I kids." If you've
worked with students, you've probably heard
or said these coded labels that reflect deficit
thinking. This focus on weakness is a perva-
sive, powerful judgment that continues to
harm students long after they leave school.
It's time for educators to hack deficit thinking. Unlearn student blame
and reframe thinking to focus on student strengths, which will help everyone reach their highest potential.

Dear Math
Why Kids Hate Math and What Teachers Can Do About It
Sarah Strong and Gigi Butterfield

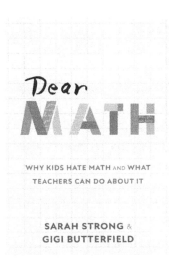

In *Dear Math*, a 15-year veteran math teacher and one of her high school students address concerns about negativity concerning math. Digging into the feelings math evoked in hundreds of middle and high school students—that math is unnecessary, oppressive, and intimidating—they explore ways to spin student expressions of unworthiness into an antidote.

Learn how to use the most important skill of all—listening—to help students discover the empowerment of math, the importance and usefulness of the subject, how to find fun instead of failure, and the beauty of mathematics in practice.

Hacking Classroom Management
10 Ideas to Help You Become the Type of Teacher They Make Movies About
Mike Roberts

Learn the ten ideas you can use today to create the classroom any great movie teacher would love. Utah English Teacher of the Year and sought-after speaker Mike Roberts brings you quick and easy classroom management Hacks that will make your classroom the place to be for all your students. He shows you how to create an amazing learning environment that makes discipline, rules, and consequences obsolete, no matter if you're a new teacher or a thirty-year veteran teacher.

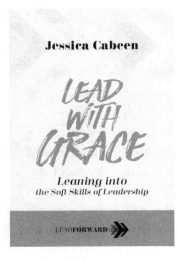

Lead With Grace
Leaning Into the Soft Skills of Leadership
Jessica Cabeen

With technology, we interact with families, students, and staff 24/7, not just during the school day. Pressures can sway who we are into one who values online likes more than the authentic interactions that establish deep relationships with those we serve. School leader and keynote speaker Jessica Cabeen offers stories and strategies, practices and exercises, to empower teachers, principals, parents, or superintendents to build confidence to lean into the soft skills of leadership and lead with grace.

Hacking Learning Centers in Grades 6–12
How to Design Small-Group Instruction to Foster Active Learning, Shared Leadership, and Student Accountability
Starr Sackstein and Karen Terwilliger

Learning centers are dynamic spaces where students can become robust thinkers, problem-solvers, and brave leaders. *Hacking Learning Centers in Grades 6–12* shares why and how to design small-group instruction that includes everyone and encourages students to collaborate, experiment, reflect, self-assess, and transfer the learning to their lives beyond school. Starr Sackstein and Karen Terwilliger show how learning centers empower unexpected leaders, raise the bar on student accountability, activate the fun to bring learning to life, and inspire students to share ideas and make decisions.

RESOURCES FROM TIMES 10 PUBLICATIONS

10Publications.com

Nurture your inner educator:
10publications.com/educatortype

Podcasts:
hacklearningpodcast.com
jamesalansturtevant.com/podcast

On Twitter:
@10Publications
@HackMyLearning
#Times10News
#RealPBL
@LeadForward2
#LeadForward
#HackLearning
#HackingLeadership
#MakeWriting
#HackingQs
#HackingSchoolDiscipline
#LeadWithGrace
#HackingSchoolLibraries

All things Times 10:
10Publications.com

TIMES 10 PUBLICATIONS provides practical solutions that busy educators can read today and use tomorrow. We bring you content from experienced teachers and leaders, and we share it through books, podcasts, webinars, articles, events, and ongoing conversations on social media. Our books and materials help turn practice into action. Stay in touch with us at 10Publications.com and follow our updates on Twitter @10Publications and #Times10News.

www.ingramcontent.com/pod-product-compliance
Lightning Source LLC
Chambersburg PA
CBHW072240290425
25937CB00028B/874